# Praise for *Finding a Purpose in the Pain*

"With great compassion, James Fenley, MD, speaks to all of us impacted by addiction, whether it is personal or within our profession. Poignantly, he addresses the basic yet profound truths that lead to and define recovery. Wherever you are in your personal or professional journey, this book will speak to you."

Claudia Black, PhD
Author of *It Will Never Happen to Me* and
*The Truth Begins with You*

"Jim Fenley's description of how he approaches the treatment of addiction as a physician is an uplifting, candid, and revealing story. Jim's understanding of addiction and recovery through his spouse and patients has been translated into his passion for helping others find their way out of the extraordinary pain of the illness. Jim has the gift of clear and understandable writing, so that this complex illness can be better understood and attacked through the concepts he shares with others. Any professional or nonprofessional with an interest in addiction and its treatment needs to have this book in their home."

Carlton Erickson, PhD
Distinguished Professor of Pharmacology/Toxicology
Director, Addiction Science Research and Education Center
College of Pharmacy
University of Texas at Austin

"Dr. Fenley combines his experience as a physician in addiction medicine and his involvement in twelve-step recovery into a fascinating and interesting book. I found the chapter on spirituality to be particularly good with the following line, 'My hope is that by accepting that they are powerless over addiction or that they are in such great emotional pain that it is impossible to make good decisions, they will look for a power source outside themselves to help guide them in their recovery.' In relationship to treatment, I see spirituality as a key element in the twelve-step model of recovery. This book provides valuable insights, not just for the individual afflicted with the disease of addiction, but also for family members of the suffering addict."

David E. Smith, MD
Founder of Haight Ashbury Free Medical Clinics of
San Francisco

"It is easy to see how Jim Fenley became the compassionate physician he is. He seems to always have that connection with patients that helps in their healing. Reading how he worked through his shame and anxiety is inspiring. He is truly an inspiration in his practice of addiction medicine, but also in his compassion for the person in need. Jim clearly found his purpose in the pain!"

Michael Fishman, MD
Director of the Young Adult Program
Talbott Recovery
Atlanta, Georgia

"*Finding a Purpose in the Pain* is an informative and entertaining book exploring the nature of addiction, its treatment, and the recovery process. The book would be an excellent reference for counselors, psychologists, and physicians who work in the treatment of substance use disorders. Many of the insights are not limited to addiction, but are relevant to a wide range of issues, people, and experiences."

Norman G. Hoffmann, PhD
Adjunct Professor of Psychology
Western Carolina University

"Jim's love and compassion for the addicted person shines through in this book, and confirms what I have always felt about him. I strongly recommend this book not only for the addict, but also for the family. You won't be disappointed."

Pat Fields
Former Administrative Director of the
Southeastern Conference on Addictive Diseases

"What an extraordinary story! Dr. Fenley's sense of warmth toward his patients who struggle with addiction is clearly evident. He has devoted his life's work to those who are stigmatized and often marginalized. He shares his own journey of recovery with those he treats, and combines science with spirituality. He clarifies the dysfunctional family in a meaningful way that will capture those who know it only too well. His own wellness guides him, and his life's story is punctuated with humor, pathos, and spiritual growth. This book is unique in its ability to reach professional staff, families of those who struggle, and the person who continues to suffer from such a complex disease.

"This book should be required reading for all medical students as well as all other clinical disciplines that treat addiction. It offers a sense of purpose and hope to a life in torment."

Donna M. White, RN, PhD, CS, CADAC
Addiction Specialist
Lemuel Shattuck Hospital

"After reading *Finding a Purpose in the Pain*, I know clearly there was a reason Dr. Fenley made addiction his vocation. His personal expression of his journey is a beacon to those who come to his doorstep exhausted by pain, fear, loneliness, and loathing. After thirty years in the addiction arena, I have come to believe that to be successful with alcoholics and addicts you have to love what you do. With Dr. Fenley, that love is made abundantly clear as you read his eloquent description of healing and recovery. This is the book I wish I could have written!"

Robert W. Mooney, MD
Medical Director
Willingway Hospital
Statesboro, Georgia

"Jim Fenley takes his personal and family history to portray his journey, which explains why he has always been so committed to helping patients understand the consequences of this disease and how recovery can provide a whole new life for them and their families. I applaud him for sharing his personal and family history, which many people would not even consider doing; but in his doing so, I think his book will help thousands."

Benjamin H. Underwood, FACHE
CEO/Managing Director
Talbott Recovery
Atlanta, Georgia

# FINDING a PURPOSE
## in the PAIN

# FINDING a PURPOSE

# in the PAIN

## A DOCTOR'S APPROACH *to* ADDICTION RECOVERY *and* HEALING

### JAMES L. FENLEY, JR., MD

CENTRAL RECOVERY PRESS

CENTRAL RECOVERY PRESS

Central Recovery Press (CRP) is committed to publishing exceptional materials addressing addiction treatment, recovery, and behavioral healthcare topics, including original and quality books, audio/visual communications, and web-based new media. Through a diverse selection of titles, we seek to contribute a broad range of unique resources for professionals, recovering individuals and their families, and the general public.

For more information, visit www.centralrecoverypress.com.

Central Recovery Press, Las Vegas, NV
© 2012 by James L. Fenley, Jr.

ISBN-13: 978-1-936290-71-0 (trade paper)
ISBN-10: 1-936290-71-5
ISBN-13: 978-1-936290-84-0 (e-book)
ISBN-10: 1-936290-84-7

18 17 16 15 14 13 12     1 2 3 4 5

Publisher:  Central Recovery Press
            3321 N. Buffalo Drive
            Las Vegas, NV 89129

**PUBLISHER'S NOTE:** The experiences and opinions expressed in this book are those of the author only. To protect their anonymity, some of the names of people and institutions have been changed.

*Cover design and interior layout by Deb Tremper, Six Penny Graphics*

This book is dedicated to my
wife, Virginia, and to my children,
Trey, David, and Elizabeth.


Most importantly, I dedicate *Finding a
Purpose in the Pain* to God, my daily source
of unfailing love, grace, strength, and peace.

# Table of Contents

# Foreword

Few physicians are better known or more accomplished than Dr. James Fenley. In more than twenty years in the practice of addiction medicine, he has become both a respected clinician and a compelling lecturer. Those colleagues who have had the privilege of hearing him speak will recall favorably his competence, intelligence, and wit. All of these attributes are on display in this work, which is a compilation of many of his educational presentations. Drawing upon his many years of experience allows him to share with the reader his unique insights into the recovery process.

With great courage, Dr. Fenley shares his personal story of overcoming depression while dealing with addiction issues within his own family. In a forthright and candid manner, he provides the reader with suggested approaches for addressing the often co-occurring issues of addiction, depression, and codependency. By identifying the problems and, in an entertaining and rational manner, offering solutions for how they can be resolved, this work is an essential tome for any healthcare professional involved in the complex field of addiction medicine. Dr. Fenley frequently offers a different way of viewing a subject that may confound the occasional healthcare professional. For example, in Chapter Eleven, "Spirituality," Dr. Fenley discusses how he has his patients associate spirituality with quiet time. He explains that a person with the disease of addiction is often "impatient and fearful of slowing down and doing things in another way." He therefore counsels his patients on how to "be still and trust a spiritual process." By internally slowing down the process, the patient gains a better grasp of the recovery process so that incremental progress can be made. It is just such offerings of alternative views on a common problem that differentiate this work from the usual treatise on the subject.

This book is a worthwhile addition to any addiction-based library and a valuable resource for those clinicians dealing with patients who present with not only the disease of addiction, but also the complicating factors of depression, codependency, and challenging family relationships that can impede the recovery process. As Dr. Fenley says, "Life is a struggle, but taken one day at a time, with a spiritual focus, it can be a path of discovery through our pain to love, freedom, and peace."

By combining the author's years of clinical experience, his personal observations, and his communication skills in a coherent and compelling literary work, this book will become a valuable resource for those involved in advancing the recovery process.

Susan K. Blank, MD, MRO, FABFE
EVP of Addiction Services
GreeneStone Muskoka
Bala, Ontario

# Acknowledgments

I would like to thank Claudia Black for being an inspiration to me since I heard her speak in 1983. She first had an impact on my life by telling me who I was in her description of childhood roles, and later by my getting to know her through her association with the Southeastern Conference on Addictive Diseases (SECAD) over the years. Her passion, her expertise in dealing with childhood trauma survivors, her smile and sense of humor, as well as her talent as an author all helped encourage me in my work with patients, and ultimately in the writing of this book. She has been a true blessing in my life.

I would also like to thank Pat Fields. Pat was the administrative coordinator for SECAD for twenty-four years. For thirteen of those years I had the privilege of working with her. Pat is loved by people in the addiction field who know her as someone with tough talk and a big heart. She has always supported me personally and professionally, and was one of the people who encouraged me to write this book. She is a class act, and I love her dearly.

I would also like to acknowledge David Smith, who has been a hero of mine in the addiction field for many years. His compassion for the addict in starting the Haight Ashbury Free Clinics at such a young age and serving as a public advocate for addiction treatment have been a source of continuing passion in my own work.

Finally, I would like to mention Dr. Bill Simpson, my mentor. I believe Bill saw something in me long before I did. Much of what I know and teach others about addiction began with him. I will never forget him.

# Introduction

*Addiction is an illness, not a moral weakness.*

In my interaction and friendships with other addiction professionals across the United States and abroad, I have so often found a connection early in our meetings. I have come to realize that this bond is usually based on our mutual passion for treating those who are sick and in need of help. We have discovered many of the same basic truths about life and recovery, although our journeys or terminology may be different.

This book is based on a series of lectures I have developed over the last twenty-six years of my addiction medicine practice. Each lecture is intended to give useful insights, coping skills, and tools that make sense and can be used in a one-day-at-a-time approach to recovery. My audiences include not only addicts, but also patients with a primary psychiatric diagnosis, nursing students, and treatment staff in general. I have found that what I initially saw as lectures geared to the addict are, in fact, often applicable to people universally, and I hope they embody the essential human truths in which I so deeply believe.

The phrase "life happens" is an accurate description of my personal history to date. I never planned to practice addiction medicine, battle chronic depression, or, least of all, write a book. I remember sitting with my therapist years ago. I had been very sad, and I think I was crying when she asked me, "What are some of the most important decisions you have made in your life?" Despite my despair, I found myself almost laughing at the question. I wanted to say, "Don't you get it?" At one time I thought that I made important decisions, but it became obvious as my adult years progressed that I was on a journey, a spiritual one, and had been for a long time. I now try to take things one day at a time. I will have periods of peace, and then something new will happen, in God's time, as I continue my work in addiction medicine.

When I was a medical student rotating on the psychiatric service, more than one of my attending physicians commented on my bedside manner and my ability to elicit trust from the psychiatric patients. But I never considered psychiatry a serious option, always feeling that I would practice internal medicine. I enjoyed the combination of taking a medical history with patient contact and solving medical diagnostic problems. By the beginning of my professional career as an internist, I had spent a lot of one-on-one time with patients. I always thought that the title of "internist" was a misnomer. The real expertise of internal medicine is in differential diagnosis—that is, taking someone's history in depth, doing a physical exam, eliminating all the diagnoses except the proper one, and treating it correctly as promptly as possible. I loved that part of medicine. The longer I practiced, the more

I learned about the true art of medicine. Two facts became very clear:

1. Nothing heals like the human touch and showing genuine caring for your patients.

2. Too many physicians fail to explain things to patients in a way they can understand.

Later, after six years of private practice in internal medicine, my wife going through her painful recovery from addiction, and my own recovery from severe depression and panic disorder, my outlook on life, medicine, and God began to change. At one point in my depression and panic, Dr. Simpson, who had been my wife's inpatient physician for her addiction treatment, admitted me to his inpatient alcohol and drug unit. He did this despite the fact that I was not an addict, with my admitting diagnosis being major depressive disorder. He thought I would feel safer under his care. As a result of this decision, I went through twelve days of inpatient addiction treatment, which, in the years to come, would give me invaluable insight into my own patients in addiction treatment. In retrospect, I don't know if Dr. Simpson had an underlying motive, but the time I spent there ultimately influenced my decision to make addiction medicine my career.

As a result of my attending recovery meetings while practicing internal medicine and directing a twelve-bed inpatient addiction unit in a med-surg hospital, my philosophy of medicine and my direction became clear. I had become aware that 60 to 70 percent of the chief complaints by patients in my outpatient internal medicine practice were at least in part emotionally based, whether it was tension headaches, chest wall pain, reflux esophagitis, restless leg syndrome, or back pain. At the same time, spirituality had become a part of my life, and I sensed that God had a plan for me. I had been to the "bottom of the pit" emotionally in my depression, and I believed I could use my experience of that pain to help others struggling with addiction.

In 1990 my wife and I made a very difficult decision to leave our friends of eleven years, my partners of eleven years, and my internal medicine practice so I could work full time in addiction medicine. This meant moving to Georgia, where we have resided since then. As I began a full-time addiction medicine practice, I felt as if I never had enough time to spend with patients one-on-one. I found that one remedy for this was to give lectures at least three days a week. I borrowed what I remembered from one or two of Dr. Simpson's lectures, and then slowly, over the years—based on patients' needs and my increased understanding of addiction—I compiled approximately twenty lectures that I routinely give. I never use notes. The lectures are just a part of who I am. By nature, I have never been research oriented or a true academic.

I don't mean to sound arrogant, but I like to think of myself in one small respect like Dr. William Silkworth. He was the treating physician for Bill Wilson, one of the cofounders of Alcoholics Anonymous. Bill Wilson called him "the little doctor who loved drunks." I love them, too. I don't know why. I just do. I'm passionate about my work, and I guess that comes through the most in my lectures and one-to-one contact with patients.

When I was chairman or cochairman of the Southeastern Conference on Addictive Diseases for many years in the 1990s and early 2000s, part of my job was to help select speakers yearly for our conference. By virtue of the conference's history, its administrative director Pat Fields, and its success, we were able to feature the brightest, best, and most respected professionals in the field of addiction medicine.

In my thirteen years there, and now my seven years serving on the planning committee for the Cape Cod Symposium on Addictive Disorders, I have witnessed a multitude of changes in our field. Two primary broad examples are philosophies of treatment with a much more positive working relationship between addiction medicine and psychiatry, and an increased focus on addiction as a brain disease. Yet, through it all, nothing has changed the basic messages of my lectures—not from my being closed-minded, but from a sense of physicians and others moving away from the simple tools and truths that I put forth. Whether I am speaking on humility, expectations, feelings, childhood roles, or finding a purpose in the pain, the need for these topics seems to increase, not decrease, over time.

The treatment I employ is primarily a combination of cognitive behavioral and twelve-step-facilitated therapy. Much attention in the cognitive behavioral area is given to coping skills. By its nature, this involves a lot of insight-oriented therapy.

I have always believed there are basically two parts to twelve-step-oriented treatment. The first is **surrendering to the pain of one's addiction** as a result of the negative consequences it has caused. The other is for the addict to begin to ask the question, "What's wrong with my thinking?" This second part involves looking at **denial and addictive thinking.** They are dealt with simultaneously as part of the treatment process. In one sense, they are approached similarly for all patients, but in another they are tailored individually to a patient's presentation, sense of safety and trust, and other considerations.

When I say that some factors are alike for all patients, what I'm alluding to are those that I believe are essential to recovery, based on the twelve-step model:

- **Becoming a good listener**

- **Being willing to take action**

- **Being honest with oneself and others**

- **Getting out of self**

Finally, becoming emotionally accountable is also critical to recovery. Patients have difficulty grasping this concept. Addicts often unconsciously take on the role of victim, or are bitter about life and blame others for their problems and how they feel. Being emotionally accountable means no longer making others responsible for your feelings, and having a willingness to risk sharing emotional pain without using mood-altering substances.

At the center of my treatment focus is spirituality. The world we live in is all about going fast, doing more with less, and constant exposure to mass media—all in a consumer-oriented culture. In treatment, I talk to patients about a God of acceptance, forgiveness, and love. Any connection to spirituality can only be made by slowing down, simplifying one's life, and spending time each day working on this spiritual connection. As with so many things in recovery, take the action and the feelings will follow.

I don't expect you to agree with everything in this book, but my hope is that it will be of help to you in some meaningful ways. As I have heard for so many years being around recovering people, "Take what you like and leave the rest."

It will be apparent in this book that little mention is made of medication. In order to prevent any misunderstanding, I feel it is important to state that medication does play a significant role in my treatment of patients in various areas of care. It is helpful and necessary in different types of medical detoxification, including patients with a diagnosis of alcohol dependence, opiate dependence, and benzodiazepine dependence. Medications are also valuable as anticraving agents, in the control of pain, and in the treatment of other coexisting medical conditions. Finally, because many of my patients have coexisting psychiatric conditions, often requiring a psychiatric consultation, psychotropic medications also play an invaluable role in the treatment of conditions such as major depressive disorder, posttraumatic stress disorder, and bipolar disorder. However, this book is about finding a purpose in the emotional pain of the patient, and therefore does not lend itself to a discussion of medications and their uses.

# CHAPTER ONE

# The Path to My Profession

*"Fear of man will prove to be a snare."*

—*Proverbs 29:25*

I was born in Bryan, Texas, in Brazos County, and was the only baby in the hospital on April 3, 1950. I was named James Lewis Fenley, Jr., but was almost named Jessie James Fenley, after my grandmother (Jessie) and my father (James). We lived in the barracks at Texas A&M University. My father was a decorated veteran of World War II, having flown in thirty-five missions in a B-17 bomber in the European Theatre, and having won the Distinguished Flying Cross. The average life expectancy of a B-17 crew in his time and area was only eight missions. After the war, while married with two small children, my father was working three jobs.

The cadets at A&M would come by and ask him about going back to school. With my mother's urging, he did. He had only finished the eleventh grade at Lufkin High School, since that was all that was offered; yet, he graduated near the top of his class, with honors in mechanical engineering, at Texas A&M.

He was the best shot I have ever seen with any kind of rifle or shotgun. He was my hero, but he was also filled with rage, and I feared him. At the same time, he was a source of real tenderness throughout my life, and I loved him dearly.

For the first ten years of my life, my family consisted of my father, my mother, and my sister, Gail. Gail, who was two years older than me, was never happy about my arrival. Looking back, I think Gail had a tough time with my mother before and after I was born, and she may have taken some of it out on me. But she was also my protector from the bigger kids when I was little. Of course, that doesn't excuse her for painting some small rocks, telling me they were candy, and asking me to swallow them. In my family, it was okay for Gail to hit, pinch, trip, or punch me, but if I punched her I got a spanking, since she was a girl.

Most of the spankings I remember getting as a child were by my father, cursing while spanking me with one hand and lifting me off the ground with his other hand. If we did something Mother didn't like, she might spank us, but either way she would call Dad, and we would wait all day and usually get a whipping when he got home. I don't remember a lot about those times. I do remember that home was a scary place for me. In our house, it seemed everyone always closed their doors. I closed mine to feel safer. I don't know why everyone else closed theirs.

My mother, Lillie May, was a mystery woman. I never knew much about her family or her childhood, while my father was always full of stories of his life on the farm with his two brothers, parents, and extended family. Any person in our neighborhood would tell you how kind and thoughtful my mother was, always going out of her way for everyone. But I don't remember much open affection, and in our house, she ruled. Dad might yell and scream, but not often at her, and afterward he always seemed to feel guilty. She was a fanatic about cleanliness. I later learned that a lot of this came from her own childhood, where her mother's flower gardens were a thing of beauty, but the inside of her house was totally uncared for until my mother became old enough to take care of it.

Our house always looked unlived in. There were never dishes in the sink, scuff marks on the floors, or pillows out of place. You had to take your shoes off at the door. When you took a bath, you were expected to clean the inside of the tub with soap and water when you were through and dry the tub, handles, curtain, and tiles. Then Mother would come immediately behind you and do it all again. I would come home from church to hang up my Sunday clothes, then I would go to the restroom, and by the time I got back Mother had already been up to my room and rehung all my clothes. I don't remember ever inviting anyone over to spend the night except maybe once when I was nine or ten years old. I couldn't imagine staying at our house being fun. I got yelled at a lot for doing things wrong or making messes from the time I was old enough to remember.

I was my mother's favorite, according to my sister. I guess it was because of my performance and accomplishments in school, sports, and music. But being her favorite certainly did not translate into a happy childhood. By the time I went to kindergarten and then grade school, I had an incredible level of anxiety, although I didn't know it. That was just normal for me. By the third or fourth grade, I would frequently throw up before school because I found that I felt better afterward. In school I was always fearful that I wouldn't know something or wouldn't do something right. I would study for a ridiculous number of hours for simple tests because of this. I don't think I made a B as a final grade on anything until I was in junior high school. In my younger years, I would sometimes cheat on tests to make sure I got 100 percent and not 97 or 98. I was miserable, and felt like an imposter. I was such a coward, so fearful of everyone, but I hid it.

My one true outlet and love was sports. I could run fast, and I grew up around a lot of boys who introduced me to baseball, football, and basketball. I loved any game that had a ball in it, but looking back, even in sports I could have been a much better athlete had I played without the fear of screwing up, which caused me to always play it safe. Still, I played for the city championship in Pee Wee Baseball for the city of Memphis, Tennessee. Our team won the junior high basketball championship for the city of Memphis, and I lettered three years in basketball and baseball in high school. Unfortunately for me, one of my coaches was like my dad, a "jersey jerker" or screamer, which didn't help my self-confidence much. My two fondest memories of sports are very different, but they have one thing in common: there was no pressure from an angry adult coach who criticized our team's play and pressured us to win.

When I was eleven years old, I lived near Avon Park, where there was one dead-end street of black families within probably a ten-mile radius. One summer some of the black boys came down to the park. I just loved playing ball, and we formed a park softball team. Our uniforms were no shirt or a T-shirt, shorts, and a baseball cap (shoes were optional). I was the only white kid, and I was the pitcher. We traveled around and played a few other park teams in some nice-looking all-white areas. Some people said things and laughed at us until the game started. Then we just "beat the stink" out of everybody. What's funny about this—and I think it is a "God-incidence"—is that five years later, when desegregation began in 1967 in Memphis and blacks were bused to my high school (ironically named White Station High School), some of the first guys off the bus were my old Avon Park softball team members, who, along with me, became a part of our high school varsity basketball team.

My second fond memory of sports came when I joined Kappa Sigma fraternity while at Vanderbilt University. Playing intramural sports was great because we coached ourselves, and I felt absolutely no pressure doing what I loved, whether it was playing linebacker or wide receiver or punter in football, point guard in basketball, striker in soccer, or third baseman in softball. I had a best friend there, Jeff Anderson, and we had an equal love of sports. He was the quarterback, and I was the leading receiver. We would have such fun working on timing and pass routes during the summer. He was the field goal kicker, and I was the holder and the punter. In softball, he was the leadoff batter and I batted second. We had a connection and a love for sports I will never forget.

I was a freshman at Vanderbilt in 1968, in the middle of the Vietnam War and everything that went with it. You could say I had an up-and-down freshman and sophomore year. As a freshman, I ended the year with a 4.0 grade point average and was accepted into the Phi Eta Sigma scholastic fraternity, a very difficult honor to achieve at that school. As a sophomore, I pledged Kappa Sigma fraternity. I discovered fraternity sports, parties, and other diversions, and actually made an F in a Southern Literature course. I never bothered to attend the class for an entire semester, including for the midterm and final exams.

I spent the rest of my college years afflicted with bouts of severe anxiety and depression. I was premed because I wasn't certain what else to be, and my father had always said it was better to be your own boss. The government reinstituted the draft, and draft numbers were assigned based on your birth date, drawn randomly "out of a hat." Each birth date was given a number from 1 to 365, according to the order in which it was drawn. The lower your number, the greater your chance of being drafted. My number was 83, which was low and meant I would probably go to Vietnam if I was not accepted to medical school. Despite my delinquent sophomore year, I recovered some balance and graduated with honors and a high GPA. However, I was drafted, went for my enlistment physical, and then, fortunately, a few days later was accepted to the University of Tennessee Medical School. I knew that my childhood neighbor and friend growing up, Seldon Feurt, PhD, Dean of Pharmacy at the University of Tennessee, had helped me through his written recommendation. He and his family had lived in the corner house on our street, and I had grown up playing with his daughters. With my lifelong feelings of being an imposter and a coward, my inability to do things right, and increasing periods of depression, I wonder how long I would have lasted in Vietnam. Maybe God had a plan for me, but I didn't see it then.

The worst part of leaving for college from high school was having to leave my brother, John, who is almost ten years younger than me. I remember running home from school, so excited, the day he came home from the hospital as an infant. He was a quiet child growing up. That would make sense in our family. I loved teaching him to play sports, and I helped coach him on teams in the summer when I was in high school and when I came home from college. He was a very good athlete. He's a psychiatrist now in Johnson City, Tennessee. I once asked him if I was a little too hard on him where sports were concerned. He said, "Let me put it this way: I think I was sixteen before I ever beat you in a game of 'horse' in basketball." Of course, that's not true, but I got the message. One thing I never did when I coached was criticize. I might have been overly vocal with my booming Irish voice, but only with words of encouragement. I had felt and seen firsthand the damage done by demeaning or humiliating athletes in front of teammates or community, and I saw no value in it.

It's interesting that my sister ended up following in my father's footsteps in the newspaper business. He was the operations manager for the *Commercial Appeal* in Memphis for over thirty years, and my sister Gail has been the editor of the *Germantown News* for twenty years. My brother started out in dental school and switched to psychiatry. I started out in internal medicine and switched to addiction medicine. I believe these career choices have something to do with our childhoods.

Most of my happiest childhood memories came from visiting Nanny. Nanny was my father's mother and lived with

Papa in a small white farmhouse at the top of a hill, completely surrounded by huge old magnolia trees, in Lufkin, East Texas (an area known as the Piney Woods). Our family would visit at least twice a year, and when we came in the summer, it was always a family reunion for my father, his two brothers, and their families. The Fenleys have the distinction of being one of the oldest pioneering families in East Texas, and we take great pride in it. There, my mother was the outsider and had no power. There, my father's rage went away, and I saw in him, as he played dominos with his father and brothers on the back porch, the boy he must have been growing up. He was full of laughter, jokes, and memories of good times.

Nanny was one of two people in my life as a child who was a source of unconditional love. I remember all the wonderful things from those early days. My cousins and I would always look forward to my dad, uncle Zack, or uncle Ray coming back from the Crystal Ice Co. with a big block of ice and a load of soda pops. They would set the ice block in a #3 washtub and break it up with an ice pick, and then jam our favorite drinks down into the ice. I remember loving soft drinks like Delaware Punch, Hires root beer, and peach and strawberry Nehi. We thought the best way to drink them after they were really cold was to leave the tops on them and punch holes in the metal tops with the ice pick. I can still taste that root beer.

Shooting cans off the fence as fast as we could with BB guns was always a fun thing to do with my cousins, because all Fenleys, male or female, were good shots. We also loved climbing the big magnolia trees. Even back then they must have been at least fifty years old. When it was too hot outside, we made a fort with overturned solid-metal outdoor chairs, with the top made of a sheet held down with clothespins.

When I was old enough I would go hunting in the woods with my dad's .22 Winchester rifle, knowing I was walking the same trails he had walked as a child with his brothers.

Nanny had worked as a nurse most of her adult life before retiring and had helped raise three boys in the height of the Great Depression. She gave great hugs, told me she loved me a lot, and never seemed to mind when I made mistakes or made a mess.

The other source of unconditional love for me was a man named Neil Hakala. He owned and ran the Central Academy of Music. When I was seven years old, my mother asked someone with which musical instrument it would be an advantage to be left-handed. The answer she received was the accordion. So my parents drove me to a somewhat run-down part of town on Jackson Avenue, and we walked into a small but well-lit store called the Central Academy of Music. There I received my first accordion lesson, and my parents purchased a blue-and-white Laurenti accordion for me. From that point until age fifteen, I took accordion lessons, although I rebelled briefly and quit once or twice along the way. I had one private lesson a week from Mr. Hakala and one accordion band lesson. That's right, a band made up entirely of accordion players.

When I think back on those years, I realize they taught me so much. First, much as with my softball teammates at Avon Park, I learned not to judge people by appearance or popularity. Let's just say our accordion band through the years was a smorgasbord of personalities, looks, and presentations. We definitely did not meet the criteria for cool or preppy, but we enjoyed each other's company and our shared love of music. Mr. Hakala was probably the kindest human being I have ever encountered. At each lesson, he never asked how much I had practiced. He just began going over the material assigned with patience and guidance. He would have his own accordion on which he demonstrated, always effortlessly, how it was to be played. He was a constant. He cared about me; he never judged, and never failed to encourage me.

When I was accepted to medical school, the University of Tennessee in Memphis decided to try a three-year instead of a four-year program. Part of what that meant was that my medical class would take only one licensing exam, called Flex, at the end of three years. God must have had a hand in this, because normally the class would have had to take the National Board Exam, Parts I, II, and III, and pass in order to graduate. By this time, while I was functioning okay day to day, I was not particularly good at taking big tests. I had experienced more than one anxiety (and probably panic) attack during tests in medical school. At the time I was unaware of what physical symptoms anxiety could produce, and what a panic attack was. As I worked my way through medical school while employed as an IV extern, starting IVs and helping out at Methodist Hospital Central, I shared an apartment with two other medical students on Peabody Avenue. On the day of my Flex exam, I ran out the front door to find the two right wheels of my car that were nearest the curb missing and the axles propped up on bricks. I am still uncertain how I made it to the test and passed the Flex exam.

I met my wife, Virginia, during my internal medicine internship and residency at the Methodist Hospital. She was the most beautiful thing I had ever seen. She had just moved back to Memphis and was seeing someone else. I remember my father commenting years later that I had said one of the things I liked the most about her was that she could be just as comfortable at a Memphis formal ball as fishing for bream in a farm pond with me. Our courtship was somewhat abbreviated. I knew she was the woman I wanted to spend the rest of my life with. To put it in the words we have both used over the past thirty-two years, we argued for three months and got married in August of 1977. Our first child, Trey, was born in July of 1978, and we moved to Jackson, Tennessee, where I joined the Medical Clinic of Jackson. It was an internal medicine group where I would practice for the next eleven years.

In 1980, my wife entered treatment for alcohol and opiate addiction. I would like to say I was the motivating force behind her getting help, but she actually sought help for herself. Not only was I was unaware of my wife's addiction when we got married, but I was also in denial of my being her chief enabler. I was convinced that if she was in recovery, everything in our family would be fine. She went through twenty-eight-day inpatient treatment, attended recovery meetings regularly, and did well until her next pregnancy with our second child, David. She was placed back on opiates during her pregnancy by her ob-gyn physician due to back and pelvic pain, and within weeks of her delivery of David, was back in treatment at Charter Lakeside Hospital in Memphis.

This time in her treatment, I participated as well. Our first family session occurred after one week of my wife's inpatient treatment. I walked in, and Virginia and her counselor, Jan, were already seated. Jan told me to take a seat opposite Virginia and to say absolutely nothing for five minutes. Then she told Virginia to talk for five minutes. That was the longest five minutes of my life. In those five minutes I learned, painfully, that I was a terrible listener, and that my wife had real difficulty carrying on a conversation. Dr. Simpson, the codirector of the program, asked Virginia and I both to attend weekly patient and family aftercare, which was an eighty-mile drive from Jackson one way. When I asked him for how long, he said, "Until I tell you to stop coming." Then he said, "Jim, some are sicker than others," and smiled. It took two years for him to tell us to stop coming.

The longer I participated in my own recovery, the more I began to consider working in the field of addiction medicine. I was fortunate in that one of my internal medicine partners, Dr. Wayne Wolfe, had been in charge of a navy detoxification unit, and I could use hours with him toward meeting the criteria to sit for a certification exam that had just begun to be offered. In 1984, I was asked by HCA Regional Hospital to serve as director of their addiction unit in Jackson while I was still practicing full-time internal medicine. I asked Dr. Simpson and Dr. Monroe about my taking the position and they said, "Fine, as long as you don't run the therapy groups yourself." So naturally, I ran the therapy groups, ran a busy internal medicine practice, and began to have panic attacks. I underwent a psychological evaluation and testing that was not very helpful.

For approximately six months, I continued to try to work, becoming more and more nonfunctional, with panic attacks occurring out of the blue more than once per day and ever-worsening depression. A panic attack for me was a hot sensation coming over my body, followed by a feeling of absolute terror; I couldn't breathe, my hands would feel numb, and I didn't know whether to be still, run, or scream. In the end, I lost forty pounds, lay in a fetal position in bed at home crying much of the time, and was eventually taken in the middle of the night to a psychiatric hospital where I stayed for three weeks.

I've never been the same person since the trauma of those six months, but at the same time, that trauma probably has in many ways made me the somewhat unique physician that I am. In treatment, I began to come to terms with allowing myself my own humanity—in other words, humility. I also looked honestly at the trauma of my childhood for the first time. The anxiety and depression I had lived with much of my life were finally being treated. I wrote letters to both my mother and father expressing my suppressed anger, fears, and hurts, and shared them with my doctor, but never mailed them. However, writing them and reading them to someone I trusted gave me a sense of relief and understanding.

In 1988 I was certified by the Society on Alcoholism and Other Drug Dependencies, later to be renamed the American Society of Addiction Medicine (ASAM), and ultimately, as a spiritual decision, left my internal medicine practice. In late 1990 I began work at Charter Lake Hospital in Macon, Georgia. I was fortunate enough around that time to meet Pat Fields, the planning coordinator for the Southeastern Conference on Addictive Diseases, one of the longest-running and best national and international addiction conferences in the country. We hit it off, and a lasting friendship was formed. I served as chairman or cochairman of that conference for thirteen years. I was a frequent speaker myself, and was able to meet some of my true heroes in the field of addiction treatment such as David Smith, Claudia Black, and Carlton Erickson.

Through all this, my days, then and now, have been routinely and by choice spent as a clinician, as I meet with addicted individuals in medical detoxification, in day treatment, and in lectures. I am one person who is lucky enough to be doing exactly what I'm supposed to be doing with my life. I realize that the gifts I have in treating patients and their families are gifts from God, and when I'm at my best I know it is not my doing. In the Bible, it talks about having treasures in jars of clay. I'm just one more jar of clay sharing my pain and wisdom, and with it, I hope, the treasure of recovery and peace of mind.

# CHAPTER TWO

# Hard Choices

*"Live like you wouldn't be afraid to sell*
*the family parrot to the town gossip."*

—Will Rogers

Recovery from addiction and the struggles of life is all about choices. Over the course of my career in addiction medicine, time and again, it has been proven to me that **the hard choice is the sober choice.** When I reflect on how I began to get an inkling of this, several things come to mind. Number one, I noticed that patients' characteristics seemed to lean toward one extreme or the other. I will discuss this in more depth later. Two, I heard myself saying to patients with ever-increasing frequency that getting into recovery is one of the hardest things they would ever do. Three, I came to believe, based on twelve-step recovery, that there are only two kinds of decisions: *addictive* decisions and *sober* decisions.

With regard to the first item, refer to the diagram below. Many years ago, I would hand out a similar diagram to each patient in treatment and have him or her mark it based on my instruction.

```
        Always angry ------ | ------ Never angry
        Always cries ------ | ------ Never cries
    Never a caretaker ------ | ------ Always a caretaker
    Saves every penny ------ | ------ Spends everything hastily
      Talks all the time ------ | ------ Never talks
     Driven to perform ------ | ------ No energy to do anything
        Always isolates ------ | ------ Never isolates
```

The diagram could be expanded using a variety of different characteristics. If the healthy attitude or means of dealing with a particular quality is represented by a vertical line, it makes sense that it would be in the middle of each horizontal line. For example, it isn't healthy to never express anger; that would mean that all of one's anger would be repressed. Nor is it healthy to be angry all of the time, since that would tend to push loved ones away and would not be reflective of all of one's true feelings. Therefore, what is healthy is somewhere in the middle. However, invariably, when I give this lecture and pick two people at random from the audience and ask each person where he or she falls along the line for a given quality, more than 90 percent of the time the person will gravitate toward one end of the line or the other.

No matter which end of the line you are near, the healthy choice is to work toward changing your natural tendency in order to reach the middle and find a balance. That means making the hard choice, and the hard choice is the sober and healthy choice.

I am unsure of the underlying reason why people tend toward one extreme or the other for certain characteristics, but ultimately the fact that life is a struggle for everyone must be at the heart of the answer. As children, unprepared for the conflict, fears, or losses we often face, we unconsciously find ways to cope and survive. It makes sense that each role we assume or choice we make regarding safety, trust, or survival will have major effects on our qualities and characteristics, thus pushing us "off center."

In inpatient treatment, good examples of patients making the hard choice are abundant. One of the most important examples involves whether a patient in group process tends to talk a lot and dominate the group or is someone who rarely speaks. The hard choice for the person who rarely speaks is to volunteer and speak up at least once during group—to be vulnerable enough to risk his or her feelings. For the person who talks all the time, the hard choice is to be silent. In both of these cases, each patient may have been unconsciously demonstrating a childhood coping skill or defense mechanism, either as a way to be safe or as a way to get needs met. The quiet individual may have learned that as a child it was safer to be "invisible" and to say nothing, and may also have difficulty identifying feelings. The talkative group member may speak about many things, but in fact is almost never vulnerable emotionally with the group. The moment he or she starts talking fast, all the emotional pain gets "stuffed" deep within. The coping skill, again, learned unconsciously in childhood, is an attempt to get needs met (for instance, to be noticed or to get approval) as well as to be safe.

Another hard choice for the patient is surrender—for example, letting go of trying to manage his or her inpatient medical detoxification and being willing to agree to some form of continuing care, be it day treatment, intensive outpatient treatment, or another level of care. Too often patients arrive with a question on their lips: "When can I leave?" This is certainly a challenge for me and others on our treatment team. I am not a believer in confrontation as a form of therapy, but I am passionate about sharing with patients the truth about addiction and the reality of their circumstances. Often when patients sit down with me for the first time, I look at them, see the muscle-wasting in their arms, the facial redness and flushing, and their trembling hands, and I say, "I'm Dr. Fenley, and you wear your disease of alcoholism on your face." These patients are usually somewhat embarrassed, but my next words are "I care about you, and I'm here to help you."

Patients will give a million reasons why they need to leave treatment early, but I remind them that there is never a "good" time for treatment.

> Addiction is defined by continued use in spite of negative consequences;[1] therefore, it makes sense that by the time a patient gets to treatment, there are usually a multitude of stressors and problems in his or her life on the outside.

One of the most common reasons for wanting to leave treatment, especially among female patients, is "I miss my children; I want to be with them, and they need me." At that point, although I empathize with a mother's love, I tell her that her desire to be home with her children is what she wants, but what they need is a clean and sober mother, and that means remaining in treatment.

Sometimes patients in treatment will say, "I've got to go!" They don't give a reason. They just have the "got to goes." In this situation, even though a person may not be thinking of using, the risk of relapse is high. The one option available outside the hospital that is not available inside the hospital is the option to use. The patient may be in denial of his or her desire to use. When the patient is in denial, the hard choice cannot be made because the addict is head-over-heels in his or her addictive thinking, and sober choices are not a reality. This is part of what makes addiction such a frightening illness.

One of the most difficult choices for addicts is staying in touch with the seriousness of their disease. Since addiction is a disease of denial, it is a daily, conscious, and difficult choice to be able to call up at a moment's notice that time when an addict's disease was most painful, frightening, or humiliating. In lecture, I often choose patients at random and ask what that moment was for them. I always give the patients the opportunity to pass and not answer, but I also remind them that the hard choice is the sober choice. Some of the answers I have received about when the disease was most painful include these:

- "Waking up in a small room with drawn curtains with a tube in my throat and a machine breathing for me. There were IV lines running out of both arms, and I couldn't speak. The last thing I remembered was being at a party and taking a lot of alcohol and pills."

- "Coming home after a four-day binge on cocaine and finding my wife and children gone, no note, and the locks on the doors changed."

- "Sitting in the back of a police car after receiving my third DUI and being involved in an accident where other people might have been injured."

- "Being alone in a motel room out of state and having no money and no one to contact; having had DTs before and knowing I had no way to get alcohol; and praying God would let me live through the withdrawal and craziness that I knew was coming."

- "Being expelled from college and charged with distribution of methamphetamines, and coming home and seeing the look and tears on my mother's face."

Staying in touch with these memories is not intended to induce shame or guilt. Remembering these moments is meant to serve as a reminder of the true face of addiction, not the fantasy or the view fostered by complacency that commonly creeps in when life begins to improve. When the sharing of these moments is completed in lecture, the room is silent, and there is a bond among those patients based on their shared pain and making the hard choice.

In this book, I have included a chapter on humility. Its message is that the journey to humility is a painful one, but one that leads to true peace of mind. I believe that part of what makes the journey to humility so difficult is the number of hard choices one must make along the way, such as hard choices involving the need to be right, the need to judge others, and the need to be in control.

Every argument is ultimately about who is right. It's like one person saying, "Did not!" and the other saying, "Did too!" If one quits saying "Did not!" or "Did too!" the argument is over, but for that to happen, the person needs to give up the need to be right. Do you realize that being right has never helped a relationship? Then why do we make it so important? I believe that for many of us, being right is a *poor excuse for injured self-esteem.* In other words, we have a big hole inside us where we don't feel good about ourselves, so being right is at least something, and over time this becomes more and more crucial to us.

Another reason for the need to be right is that if we make the rules, then no one can back us into a corner with our feelings. It is an extremely hard choice to give up the need to be right, but once it is done, it frees us spiritually, simplifies life, and decreases conflict.

Another example of a hard choice is to stop judging people. As long as our attention is on others, on criticizing or belittling them, we don't have to look honestly at our own actions and motives. When we make the hard choice and stop judging others, we keep our primary attention on self. While this may initially be frightening and painful, it allows for important changes in attitude and emotional growth.

My last example of a hard choice is giving up the need to control. Many of the intrinsic reasons for the need to control are similar to the reasons for the need to be right. I believe many of us think that if we manage well, we will be successful and happy. It has often been my experience in treating psychiatric patients with depression, addicts, and people in general that control is in many ways an illusion. While in the workplace being organized, prepared, and efficient pays dividends, in life there often seems a proportional relationship between the amount of control someone exerts and the amount of conflict and fear in his or her personal life. For some people, to feel out of control must be avoided at all costs. But for these individuals, giving up control is actually the healthy choice (spiritually), and the fear is replaced with a sense of calm and peace over time.

Finally, I have one more anecdote to share where hard choices are concerned. I was getting ready to leave the psychiatric hospital in early 1985 after my hospitalization with major depression with panic disorder. I was going to make a hard choice and stop by to see Dr. Bill Simpson, the director of the Addictive Disease Program. He was my mentor in addiction medicine. I knocked on his door. In his usual gruff voice, he said, "Come in." Bill was probably six-foot-one or six-foot-two and weighed two hundred pounds, with long, graying hair and a long, straight, gray beard. I walked in and said, "Hi, Bill. I want to tell you something." Never rising from his chair behind his desk, he said in typical Bill fashion, "Well, what is it?" I said, in a somewhat hesitant voice, "I love you." He said, "That's not what you mean." Embarrassed now, I said, "Well, thank you." He said, "That's not what you mean either." By this time I was sitting in the chair opposite his desk, and he rolled his chair around, without getting out of it, until he was facing me. He put his hands on my knees, looked me in the eyes and said, "What you really mean is, 'Will you love me?' Jim, you've spent your life going and doing for others, being a caretaker and an enabler, showing people how much you care because it's easier for you to do all of that than it is for you to ask one person to care for you." When he finished speaking, I cried, and he hugged me. Since then, I've tried to make that hard choice to ask people to care for me, and have shared that story with thousands of family members of addicts and other "caretakers" in the hope that they, too, will make the same hard choice.

Being in recovery means doing the opposite of addictive behavior. This requires awareness, commitment, a program that works, and taking life one day at a time. Listed in the following table are typical characteristics of addictive thinking and behavior in the left column, and the opposite—twelve-step-based philosophies—in the right column.

| Addiction | Recovery |
|---|---|
| Going fast | Slowing down |
| Isolation | Fellowship |
| Impatience | Trusting the process |
| Managing your own addiction | Trusting God daily |
| Blaming others | Changing yourself |
| Needing problems | Seeking serenity |
| Into self; selfish | Out of self; selfless |
| Asking, "Why me?" | Acceptance |
| Drawn to conflict | Keeping life simple |
| Bitter; victim of yesterday | One among others; just for today |

When we look at these comparisons, there can be little doubt that (1) twelve-step recovery clearly addresses each aspect of addictive thinking and behavior, and (2) getting into recovery is about making the hard choice, one day at a time.

Relapse prevention is an area that involves making hard choices. One of the first and hardest choices for the addict is often giving up "old places and old friends." The term *friends* is probably not the best characterization here, because these kinds of friends will always choose the substance or addictive behavior in the end. Another hard choice in relapse prevention is going to daily recovery meetings and getting and making daily contact with a sponsor. A third hard choice in relapse prevention is accepting that a "drug is a drug is a drug." In other words, if you are addicted to, for example, opiates, you cannot use any other addictive substances (except in certain cases such as medical emergencies or other physician-directed circumstances).

If in the treatment of your addiction you have been fortunate enough to have been educated about cross-addictions or substitute addictions, the hard choice here involves understanding that you cannot continue in your gambling addiction while working on your recovery from drug addiction. The dynamics and behaviors of any manifestation of addiction are the same, and the likelihood of staying in recovery from one addictive behavior is very small if you remain active in another.

So where is the proof of these insights I've shared, that making the hard choice works? I've done this clinical work for enough years now that I often run into people I've treated in the past. On one such occasion I was in a restaurant, and as I walked up to pay, the cook approached me and asked, "Dr.

Fenley, do you remember me?" "Honestly," I responded, "I remember your face, but not your name." He told me his name and then said, "I've got seven years in recovery, my family has been restored to me, I've got this job, and I'm still making the hard choices."

## Chapter Two Notes

1. American Psychiatric Association, *Diagnostic and Statistical Manual of Mental Disorders (DSM-IV)*, Fourth Edition (Arlington, VA: American Psychiatric Publishing, 2000).

# CHAPTER THREE

# Addictive Thinking and Surrender

*Addictive thinking is a form of denial.*

As the years began to pass in my career in addiction medicine, I began to see recovery as having two separate, vital pieces. The first is the act of surrender, where the addict recognizes that he or she has an illness over which he or she is powerless and that has taken control of his or her life. In the second piece of recovery the addict begins to ask the question, "What's wrong with my thinking?"—in other words, identifying addictive thinking.

Surrendering to one's addiction is always a painful process. It means addressing the emotional pain of the disease. In effect, the addict has been medicating his or her feelings for a long time. Because feelings are automatic, we don't get to choose what we feel or whether we feel. The emotions that are contained deep inside the active addict are never happiness, joy, and excitement, but instead are hurt, anger, and fear.

**To admit one's disease, his or her addiction, and to look clearly at the devastation it has caused, is also to feel long-repressed emotional pain.**

There is the fear that once the alcohol or other drug or the addictive behavior is gone, what is left? What will be left of the person I once was? There is also the overwhelming fear of the unknown and learning to be emotionally accountable for oneself. In the previous chapter I talked about emotional accountability and its meaning. At its essence, it is no longer blaming others for your feelings or the problems in your life. It means accepting that your feelings are your own. Too often I see patients admitted into the hospital for detoxification from alcohol or other drugs, and they recognize the need to quit for a variety of often serious reasons. Examples include fear of losing their marriage, their children, their physical health, or their job or career, or fear of serious legal issues. Yet recognizing the need to quit does not equal surrender.

**Just having a good enough reason to quit never got anyone sober.**

I remember a young man, whom I'll call Frank, who by his early thirties already had cirrhosis of the liver from his alcoholism, and as a complication of this had esophageal varices. These are distended tiny veins in the esophagus (or swallowing tube) that are prone to bleeding and can be life-threatening. This esophageal bleeding had happened to Frank several times, and each time, after a near-fatal bleed, he would be admitted into my care for medical detoxification. He always said he would never drink again because he didn't want to die, but he never surrendered to his alcoholism, continued to rely only on willpower, and finally, despite everyone's efforts, died from another bleeding episode.

When someone relies on just having a good reason to quit, he or she is usually relying on willpower alone. After so many years of treating this illness, it is my belief that willpower alone is seldom enough.

When talking to my patients in lecture about surrender, I'm always reminded of what my mentor, Dr. Bill Simpson, used to say. When the subject of major changes in our lives came up, including surrendering to being powerless over addiction, Bill would simply say, "We all go down screaming." When he first said that to me, I felt a chill inside, and I thought, "What a graphic, almost violent statement." But over the years I have come to understand what he meant. We as human beings hold onto what is familiar, even if it is painful and destructive, because our fear of the unknown is so great. Unfortunately, for most of us, it often takes circumstances becoming so painful that "anything has got to be better than this" before we are finally willing to take a leap of faith and trust that something or somebody will be there for us.

When patients in inpatient treatment surrender and share honestly during group process that they are addicts and recount some of the things they have done in their addiction, much to their surprise, instead of rejecting them or seeing them as weak, the group reaches out to literally embrace them. They speak of the patients' courage, identifying with their losses and their emotional pain. They express their concern and care, not judging the patients, but welcoming them into a new place in their recovery, a place where they can find peace. It's always interesting to me that I can usually tell when this has happened when I see patients the morning after on rounds. There is softness in their faces, the worry lines are gone, the general tension has dissipated, and there is a good kind of exhaustion that they carry with them. This "good kind of tired" comes from letting go of a lot of the old baggage of denial, dishonesty, and pain. It is always wonderful to see.

Some patients surrender prior to admission to the hospital and are admitted while actively "bleeding emotionally." Such patients need immediate attention in the form intensive individual work, for they are hungry for recovery and ready to rid themselves of the pain of their addiction. There are many ways to do this, but I have always believed that written assignments, to be completed overnight and shared with me the next day, are some of the most effective ones. Depending on the patient's issues, the assignments may vary. However, I am very clear as to how the assignment is to be done. I ask the patient to complete it in one sitting—no rewrites, no editing. If the assignment is to write a letter to a person, living or dead, I ask the patient to write it as if this were his or her one chance to say everything he or she needed to say to that person. I let the patient know that the letter will not be mailed. I ask the patient not to reread that assignment when it is finished, but to fold it up and not look at it again until it is handed to me the following morning. Then I will read it to him or her.

Topics for the letter assignment have included

- Saying good-bye to your addiction

- Writing a letter to the person you've hurt the most in your addiction other than yourself

- Writing a letter telling me who you are (not what you do, but your authentic self)

- Making a list of your old rules for living that don't seem to be working for you anymore (many of these old rules are not your own)

- Writing a letter to a deceased spouse, not to say good-bye but to reopen communication, to remember the good times, and to move past the grief

- Describing a particularly painful day in your childhood

It is up to the expertise of the treating professional to know which assignment is most appropriate without being too overwhelming. For instance, in the case of making a list of old rules that aren't working anymore, the patient who would benefit from this assignment the most is the addict who is self-critical, has difficulty accepting his or her addiction as a disease, and often is living by rules of a critical parent's voice or parents' expectations that help foster a sense of failure and poor self-esteem. By identifying these old rules and their origin, the patient may be able to gain the insights to stop giving power to someone else's rules, and begin to make a new list of rules that are supportive of recovery, allowing him- or herself and his or her parents their own humanity by doing so.

One further way of knowing if a person has truly surrendered to being powerless over his or her addiction is if he or she believes without doubt that there is not a problem in this world that a drink or a drug won't make worse. Looking at powerlessness in these terms, there is a clear statement that the addict no longer sees a drink or a drug as anything but a path to destruction.

For me, surrender meant actively seeking God, finally letting go of control, and crying out for help. A God of Grace heard me, and slowly, day by day, in small ways and through other people and prayer, lifted me out of the "pit." It is not the same for everyone. I believe every addict has that one moment of truly jumping off the cliff as an act of surrender, but since recovery is a one-day-at-a-time process, the addict must recommit to being powerless on a daily basis if recovery is to be maintained.

**Denial is when someone subconsciously convinces him- or herself something isn't true when it is, or that something is true when it is not.**

The second major part of recovery, addictive thinking, is synonymous with denial. Anytime an addict is engaged in addictive thinking, he or she is in some form of denial. For example, let's assume I'm taking a history from Carl, a forty-nine-year-old Caucasian male, and part of his history includes his twenty-year daily drinking habit of a pint or more of liquor; six DUIs, all related to alcohol; cirrhosis of the liver (alcohol related); and two marriages that ended due to his drinking. I have already explained to Carl that the heart of the definition of addiction is a history of continued use despite negative life consequences. Then I ask Carl, "Are you an alcoholic?" and he looks me straight in the eyes and believes himself when he answers, "No sir, I'm not." That is denial. Now, if I took this same history from Carl and asked the same question, and Carl thought to himself, "Yes, I'm an alcoholic, but I'll be damned if I'll tell him," and then answered, "No, I'm not"—that is not denial. That is dishonesty. Denial is part of what makes this potentially fatal illness so frightening and dangerous.

I have a background in art therapy, and I sometimes use art therapy with my patients. It can be a wonderful means of illustrating denial. I give patients a blank white sheet of paper and a set of ten crayons and ask them to draw a picture of the pain of their addiction. I tell them not to collaborate with other patients on their drawings, and intentionally give no other specific instructions. The following are some examples of how denial can be demonstrated in this format.

1.  A patient denies having a big ego or control issues, but his drawing is dominated by a huge, detailed picture of himself with a lot of written description of the meaning of his drawing. The large self-portrait speaks to his increased ego,

and the detailed nature of his drawing and the
need to write down the meaning of the artwork
both speak to control.

2.  A patient states that she no longer sees using
    drugs as an option. The objects in her drawing
    include a crack house, wasted syringes, empty
    pill bottles, the hospital where she used to work,
    and her children; yet, the colors she chooses
    to illustrate this with are green, yellow, orange,
    and purple. These are happy colors compared
    to black, red, or blue, which more often denote
    sadness, anger, violence, and depression. Her
    choice of colors speaks to her denial, lack of
    surrender, and continued positive memories
    about using.

I often review the products of art therapy in a group setting,
both to reinforce the painful honesty of some of the drawings
and to give patients the opportunity to share with the group
their intentions related to their drawings. I then point out the
denial, not in a judgmental way, but in a caring but serious
manner for all to see its power.

Abraham Twerski is a rabbi from Pittsburgh, Pennsylvania,
who runs an addiction rehabilitation center. He is a gifted
speaker, and his favorite topic is addictive thinking. The
first time I heard him speak, he began to talk about Aristotle
and Aristotelian syllogisms. He explained that with these
syllogisms, there would be a major premise, a minor premise,
and a conclusion. This set of statements represented man's
first example of formal logic. Then Rabbi Twerski would

demonstrate addictive thinking using this reasoning. A normal person would, for instance, say:

> Major premise: All humans are mortal.
>
> Minor premise: All Southerners are human.
>
> Conclusion: All Southerners are mortal.

An addict would say:

> Major premise: All humans are mortal.
>
> Minor premise: All Southerners are human.
>
> Conclusion: I need a drink.

Laughter has to be a part of treating this illness, and nowhere is it more evident than in talking about addictive thinking. For example, consider the alcoholic who was heavily intoxicated, had a head-on collision with a tree, stumbled from the totaled car, and, with slurred speech, said in all sincerity, "I've got to stop driving." Or the methamphetamine addict in the exact same situation, who, after having such a collision, limped from the car with a smile on his face and said, "Boy, I'm glad that wasn't my car." Such is the gravity of denial and the potentially fatal fantasy world of active addiction.

In the chapter on hard choices, I listed characteristics typical of addictive thinking. One of the most prominent is to externalize problems, to blame things on other people or situations. This tendency to play the role of victim and/or to be bitter about what life has "done to" him or her is totally unconscious on the part of the addict and is part of the denial system. Those addicts who have an easier time expressing hurt outwardly invariably take on the role of victim, while those who express anger outwardly with greater ease take on the role of being bitter or angry. The unconscious reward in this for chemically dependent individuals is that they never have to look at themselves, and therefore, never have to quit using substances.

Another dominant aspect of addictive thinking is extreme self-centeredness. Remember, these are qualities of the addict in his or her active disease, not necessarily qualities of the person outside his or her addiction. This selfishness occurs as the addictive behaviors become more and more the central feature of the addict's life, to the point where other priorities, such as family, health, work, and God, are slowly pushed away. The addict can't see it, but once head-over-heels in addiction, he or she is the center of the universe, accompanied by his or her best friend (alcohol and/or other drugs), which inevitably turns on the addict at some point with devastating results. By this point, the addict is isolated and only "living to use and using to live." The reward center in the brain is damaged, as is the world around the addict.

An additional aspect of addictive thinking is impatience. Addicts want what they want when they want it, and will say whatever they have to say in order to get it. Many addicts also seem addicted to danger, excitement, and impulsive behavior. It is all about changing the way they feel right now, regardless of the consequences. With this impatience comes the behavior of saying or doing whatever the addict has to in order to get the drug. All this perpetuates the "going fast" aspect of addiction and the loss of control that can lead to fatal consequences.

The natural inclination with addictive thinking is to repeat the same act over and over and over again. Also inherent in addictive thinking is the belief that the addict can manage his or her addictive behavior. For example, the alcoholic in denial believes over and over, "This time when I drink, it will feel just as good as it once did and won't cause any problems." The power of denial is amazing. I remember talking to two married friends of mine, whom I'll call Claire and Tom, years ago after a recovery meeting. Claire had been a recovering spouse for eighteen years, and Tom had been in recovery for ten years. Claire happened to mention a Christmas she and her husband had attended at her parents' years earlier in Chicago. She could say only a few words before Tom interrupted to say what a wonderful Christmas it had been and what a great time he and Claire had had. Claire looked at him as if he had lost his mind. She then proceeded to remind him that he was drunk the entire time, humiliated her in front of her family, and actually fell into the Christmas tree, crushing it and everything around it. Tom's only response was "Really?"

Another part of addictive thinking is a need for problems. As long as an addict has a problem, he or she has a reason to use. Of course, addicts are unaware of this need because of denial, but they always seem to be in conflict with something or somebody.

Just because an addict enters some form of treatment and verbalizes that he or she is an addict does not mean it is an end to addictive thinking. In early recovery, even the most dedicated person will go in and out of addictive thinking on a daily basis. That is why it is so important for the addict in early recovery to attend daily recovery meetings, get a sponsor, and read recovery-approved literature. The more that a person hears, sees, and models recovery-oriented thinking and behavior, the less denial—and with that, addictive thinking— is likely to play a role in his or her life.

Sometimes when giving my lectures I'm accused of being a little too hard-nosed or rigid. I don't allow patients to be late. I don't allow cross talk, and I don't allow people to sleep or slouch in their chairs. I guess the reason for that is that with addiction, no one knows when the ditch may become a canyon overnight. One wrong step, and a life could be ended. I look out at an audience of inpatients, and when I see a lack of seriousness generally among them, I remind them that addiction can be a fatal illness. Then I usually tell them the story about the preacher in the flash flood:

A preacher is standing on a rooftop, knee-deep in water, when a rescue boat full of people comes by. Someone from the boat yells, "Preacher, get in or you'll drown." The preacher answers, "No, I'm a child of God; I've spent my whole life in His service. He promised to take care of me. You folks just go on." After more fruitless requests from the passengers for him to board, the boat leaves. Fifteen minutes later, the water is past the preacher's waist and another boat approaches. A man yells, "Preacher, we're the last boat. Get in or you will surely drown." "No! No!" says the preacher. "God will save me. Go on and leave me be." The boat reluctantly moves on. Ten minutes later, with the preacher barely able to keep his head above water, a helicopter appears overhead and throws down a rope ladder within easy reach of his hand. A voice from the helicopter yells, "Grab hold and we'll pull you up. We're low on fuel, but we'll save you." The preacher shouts back, "No, save yourselves. I'm fine. I'm a man of God and he promised to take care of me. You go on." The helicopter raises the ladder, turns, and disappears. Five minutes later the preacher drowns. He arrives in heaven and demands an audience with God and is given one. Standing before the Almighty, the preacher says, "Lord, I don't understand. I have had unwavering faith in you, I have given my life to you, and you promised you would help me in my hour of need. Why didn't you?" God answered, "What do you want? I sent you two boats and a helicopter!"

Each day as I look out at a new group of patients, I remember that story and want them to understand that there's no guarantee there will be another moment of clarity (another boat or helicopter) before they could drown in the dark waters of denial and addictive thinking. It is a patient's responsibility to take action and jump in the boat of recovery.

# CHAPTER FOUR

# Feelings

*"There can be no transforming of
darkness into light and of apathy into
movement without emotions."**

——

—*Carl Jung*

**W**hen I look back at my childhood now, some feelings are obvious to me. There was my father's and sister's frequent anger and my constant fear and periods of sadness. However, somehow, as I grew up I managed to unconsciously repress my own feelings to the point of having serious difficulty identifying them. While I was unaware of it at the time, I apparently needed to be in control and

---

* From *The Collected Works of C. G. Jung,* © 1961 Princeton University Press. Used by permission.

stay constantly busy as a way of not feeling anything. By the time my wife entered treatment in 1980, I was an extremely controlling husband who was convinced the only problem in our marriage was her addiction.

I remember attending my first patient aftercare meeting led by Helen Simpson, the wife of Dr. Bill Simpson, codirector of addiction treatment at Charter Lakeside Hospital. She checked in with each family member and asked how he or she was feeling. When she asked me, I said something like "I feel like Virginia is doing well." She responded, "That is what you think, not what you feel." Then I said, "Well, I feel being here will be helpful to me." She responded again, "That is what you think, not what you feel." After several more minutes of this, I was able to identify that I felt "uncomfortable." This feelings stuff was new to me, and I didn't like it.

These meetings took place weekly, and two weeks later another woman was talking about her husband and what a wonderful person he was except when he was drinking. That didn't make much sense to me because from what I could understand, her husband had been constantly drinking for the entire twenty years of their marriage. Exasperated, I muttered under my breath, "bull****," certain that no one heard me. Wrong again. Helen Simpson immediately looked at me and asked, "What did you say?" I did not respond, but my heart began to race and I began to sweat. She kept asking, and finally I answered and told the group without much eye contact that I had said "bull****." I then walked out of the group room into the men's restroom, vomited, and stood there shaking in front of the mirror, feeling totally out of control. I'm not sure to this day what made me go back to that group room a few minutes later, but I did. I talked about what happened, and from that evening forward, group became a much safer place for me. I realized that people had seen me at my worst, and when I risked sharing my feelings, they reached out to comfort and encourage me.

There are several other instances and people who have influenced my recovery where my understanding and philosophy regarding feelings are concerned. Even so, my views and convictions with respect to feelings come primarily from Jan Lowery, who is no longer with us and whom I miss greatly. In the mid-1980s, Jan ran a practice in Memphis, Tennessee, called the Gestalt Institute. My wife and I had first met Jan years earlier as part of our couples work in early recovery. We joined Jan's therapy group and were exposed to psychodrama and experiential therapy for the first time. Without explaining these methods of treatment, let me say that they can involve role playing, reliving and acting out past painful memories, and becoming more aware of your body and its symptoms as an expression of underlying feelings.

By far, the most important belief that Jan established with members of the group was that there are basically four core feelings that are present at birth: joy, hurt, anger, and fear. A newborn infant is capable of expressing each of these. A baby can coo and smile to express joy, and has a cry for anger that is different from a cry that expresses hurt. Finally, when a doctor claps his hands above a newborn to check the "startle reflex," the baby experiences fear.

**There are basically four core
feelings that are present at birth:
joy, hurt, anger, and fear.**

Why is the belief that there are only four core feelings so important? Let me explain. We live in a world with a multitude of words that signify feelings that are negative in connotation—words such as *embarrassed, guilty, ashamed, frustrated, anxious, nervous, desperate, depressed, self-pitying, humiliated, annoyed*, and many more. What's interesting is that we are not born with any of these feelings. We are taught these words as we grow up. We learn what it means to feel guilty, to feel self-pity, or to feel ashamed. When we feel one of these feelings, what do we do with it? It weighs us down, and we can often be trapped in that feeling. But if we look beneath a feeling such as shame, we will invariably find one or more of three core feelings: anger, fear, or hurt. If we risk expressing one or more of these core feelings outwardly, there can be emotional relief, which, in large part, is the major goal of therapy.

To understand this better, let's look at some basic characteristics of feelings, and then at the relationship between the feelings of anger and hurt in a given individual.

### Characteristics of Feelings

1. **All feelings are automatic.** We do not get to choose our feelings, but we do have some choice as to how we deal with them. In other words, just because feelings are automatic does not mean that we are at liberty to express them in an inappropriate way. Also, as we will learn in relation to the feelings of hurt and anger, the fact that feelings are automatic does not necessarily mean that we identify a feeling at the time it

occurs. Also, the emotion we outwardly express may not be a true reflection of our initial feeling.

2.  Because feelings are automatic, then **all feelings are okay.** How we express them may not be appropriate, but the core feelings are okay and part of being human. This comes up often as an issue with patients. A good example is someone who expresses feelings of hatred toward a parent, but then feels guilty because he shouldn't feel that way about his father. I try to explain to patients, first, that the opposite of love is not hate, but to be discounted. To have feelings of hatred, you have to care about someone. Plus, pretending that a feeling doesn't exist or that you shouldn't feel a certain way accomplishes nothing. Feelings do not disappear. I would try to convince the patient in the example that only by owning his hatred or anger and working through it is he ever going to arrive at a place of acceptance and increased peace. While the relationship may not improve, he will likely have more of a sense of understanding or closure. Also, in the process, he is likely to find a considerable amount of unrealized hurt and fear beneath the anger.

3.  **Feelings are neither moral nor immoral.** We live in a world where we frequently hear, "You shouldn't feel that way," which implies

judgment and takes feelings into the realm of morality. Being told how we should feel about a particular situation contradicts both feelings being automatic and that all feelings are okay. Too often patients of mine who struggle with self-esteem still hear that critical voice from childhood with all the "shouldn'ts" and "supposed tos" in their heads, constantly making them question their decision making and feelings.

4.  **Our feelings are our own.** No person can make you feel a certain way. Too often, people in general, and particularly addicts in their disease, blame others for how they feel. The way I typically disprove this in lecture is to pick someone at random—let's say a patient named Wade. Then I present two scenarios. In the first, Wade is called out of lecture to the telephone and finds out he just inherited four million dollars from an unknown distant relative. When he walks back in to take a seat, the person behind him pulls his chair out from under him. When I ask the group how much that is likely to bother him at that moment, they often laugh and answer, "Not much." Then, in the second scenario, Wade is called to answer the phone and has an unpleasant conversation with his wife. Again, when he comes back to sit down in lecture, his chair is pulled out from under him. Needless to say, his reaction is quite different.

The person pulling the chair out did the same thing in each instance, but Wade was in a totally different place emotionally when each action occurred, and that determined his response in the two situations. I am not saying people and events do not have an effect on our feelings, but our feelings are our own.

**It is my belief that we learn early on as children (by age three to five) that it is either not okay to express anger outwardly or not okay to express hurt outwardly. Since feelings are automatic, it's as if each person develops a switch inside. If anger is not okay, when anger comes in, the switch is flipped and the anger is either unexpressed altogether or ends up coming out as hurt, which is okay for this person to express outwardly. If hurt is not okay for a given person, and that emotion comes in, again, the switch is flipped and it is either never expressed or is outwardly manifested as anger.**

## Hurt and Anger

When discussing hurt and anger in lecture, I ask everyone who has an easier time expressing anger outwardly to raise their hands and keep them up. I then tell everyone with their hand up that the main feeling they need to work on in treatment is their unexpressed hurt. After that, I repeat the process with those who more easily express hurt outwardly and explain that it is their unexpressed anger that should be their primary focus. This relationship between hurt and anger surfaces in many important ways in treatment of addiction.

Patients with major depressive disorder who express hurt more easily fit the old adage that "depression is often anger turned inward." They will typically present with crying spells or feelings of lack of joy, sadness, being easily overwhelmed, and so forth. On the other hand, for those patients who express anger more easily than hurt, they often present not with sadness but with anger, irritability, and intolerance.

For patients for whom anger is okay but hurt is not, it is important to remember that not all depression is sadness. Often this second kind of depression is missed, since its presentation is atypical. Interestingly, also in my own experience with this type of depression, the more underlying hurt I am able to bring to the surface, the less anger remains and the greater the improvement in the depression.

**The price we pay for always trying to be safe emotionally is loneliness.**

## Joy

It may be obvious by now that one of the core feelings has been given no attention. That feeling is joy. Unfortunately, when addicts come into treatment, joy is not a part of the history that we hear or a part of the pain of their addiction. We do, however, remind patients that recovery is a process, and when patients go out to recovery meetings for the first time and see those with long-term recovery laughing and joking before and after meetings, they are often amazed. Sometimes a patient gets angry, thinking the people at the meeting are not taking recovery seriously. I explain that taking recovery seriously allows someone to laugh again, but during the meeting, while there may be humor, the message is sincere and heartfelt.

## Fear

Fear is often the feeling that is with us the most. When I think of fear, first and foremost I remember my childhood, and then my fear surrounding Virginia's addiction, and finally my fear as just another struggling human being. At one time in my life, part of my fear was due to a chemical imbalance associated with my panic attacks and major depressive disorder back in 1984. Fear was a constant companion for me as a child, either fear of my father's anger or fear of failure.

Over the years, I have discovered that the issue is more basic than a fear of failure. *It is a fear of doing something wrong.* I have found this basic fear to be very common among my addicted patients, but they could not have found the right words to express it. For me, there is no doubt that my level of fear is most affected by my faith and ability to let go and let God. The more fear I have, almost assuredly, the more I am back in the driver's seat trying to control everything—most of which I have absolutely no ability to influence or change. When I'm in that place, I always have this picture of myself in front of a twenty-foot-high, eight-foot-thick stone wall with only a chisel and a hammer in my hand and the belief I must break through the wall today. So I work constantly from dawn to dusk until my hands are bloody and sheer exhaustion forces me to stop. As I fall down, I look behind me, and there is God sitting atop a huge piece of machinery with a wrecking ball, waiting patiently for me to get out of His way.

While this will be dealt with more in the chapter on childhood roles, fear has often been with us since an early age. This may be fear of abandonment, fear of when the next screaming match or attack will come, fear based on mistrust from repeated disappointments, or fear from never feeling safe.

One characteristic of fear is that when you keep it to yourself, it just gets bigger and bigger. You tend to assume the worst or, as I say, "awfulize" potential situations. This is particularly true in the midst of depression. Therefore, one of the most important solutions to dealing with fear is to tell someone. Don't keep it to yourself. We all have fears. By sharing yours with others, you are giving everyone a gift, and making it easier for someone else to risk sharing about his or her own fear.

I talked earlier about taking the risk of expressing underlying core feelings as a way of obtaining emotional relief. For the person who represses anger, it is taking a risk to share his or her anger and/or fear that brings relief. For the person who represses hurt, it is taking a risk to share his or her hurt and/ or fear that brings relief.

So much of getting and staying in recovery is about learning to live life one day at a time. This includes slowing down and having quiet time, which helps us connect with our emotional pain, with the help of professionals when needed.

**When it comes to your addiction,
you're the last person to know
what's best for you.**

I also believe that when people are in deep emotional pain, such as in the midst of a major depression, they are the last ones to know what is best for them, for all they can feel is the pain. I have been to the bottom of the "pit" of that kind of depression and know that to be true. In those times, you must trust others, take the actions that are asked of you, and trust and pray that better feelings will follow in time—and they will.

# CHAPTER FIVE

# Resentments

*"Those who are free of resentful
thoughts surely find peace."*

—*The Buddha*

Resentment has long been considered the number-one cause of relapse. Why is that true, and what is a resentment? When I ask a group of inpatients these questions, I get a variety of answers. Perhaps a simple definition is to say it is a grudge. A resentment is something typically associated with anger, that smolders over time, regarding a certain person, persons, or situation that one just can't seem to release. The reason this is the number-one cause of relapse is that what an addict needs more than anything else to stay active in his or her addiction, other than a drink or a drug, is a *problem*! One good resentment can last a lifetime, and can unconsciously be a reason to continue to engage in addictive behavior. At the heart of addictive thinking is the need to externalize problems. Therefore, the addict never has to look at him- or herself. A resentment certainly accomplishes that. Furthermore, resentments are a natural part of what happens in the addicted family. This is explained in greater detail in Chapter Twelve, "The Addict and the Chief Enabler."

Having met with and treated inpatient addicts individually for over twenty-five years, I learned early on to ask patients to write a resentment list. It serves as a means of identifying their resentments and understanding some of their core issues. It may also be a first attempt for them to risk expressing their feelings in written form. However, as with any written task I ask a patient to do, there are specific instructions for how it is to be done.

The feeling most associated with resentment is anger. I ask patients to make a list of resentments from birth to present, and to do it in one sitting. I also ask them to write down each resentment as a complete sentence, and I state clearly that none of the resentments can be self-directed. The resentment may be directed toward a person, persons, or situation. There may be multiple resentments toward a single individual. The list would look something like this:

1. I resent my brother because when I was ten years old he took my school money and I felt betrayed.

2. I resented moving to Chicago when I was twelve because I had to leave all my friends.

The longer the list, the better. When the list is finished, I ask each patient who outwardly expresses anger more easily than hurt to put a checkmark by the one, two, or three resentments that still stimulate the most anger. Then I ask the patient to go back through the list, one resentment at a time, and put an asterisk by any resentment where he or she can identify underlying hurt.

When I started asking patients to write resentment lists many years ago, I found almost one-half of my patients either could not or would not do this. At first I thought perhaps the addicts who were used to playing the victim role in their addiction were just not willing to own their resentments or anger because it might interfere with them being seen as fragile by their enablers or treating professionals. While there is some truth to that, it was many years later when the real reason came to me. It wasn't that most of these patients were unwilling to do a resentment list; it was that they couldn't identify resentments because they didn't "do" anger. As I explained in Chapter Four, "Feelings," most of us have an easier time expressing either anger outwardly or hurt outwardly, but not both. We learn unconsciously early on as children that one or the other is not okay. Feelings are automatic; therefore, if I tend to express hurt outwardly, then when the feeling of anger appears inside me, a switch gets flipped, hurt comes out, and the anger is internalized and unexpressed.

Once I realized this truth, I began to have those patients write a list of hurts rather than resentments. They have no more difficulty making a long list of hurts than those who tend to express anger have making a long list of resentments.

The format is the same: complete sentences that include "because." For example:

1.  When I was six years old and my first-grade teacher yelled at me for not listening, I was hurt because it embarrassed me in front of the class.

2.  When my father missed my high school graduation, I was hurt because it was important to me.

When their list is complete, I ask patients to put a check mark by the hurts that are most intense and an asterisk by each hurt where they can identify underlying anger.

If you as a reader are considering whether to try this exercise or not, ask yourself this: if you were an inpatient treatment provider working with a new patient and you knew none of her history, and she completed a thorough resentment list and then shared it with you, how well would you know her based on this one exercise? Her resentment list would provide me, as her physician, with a wealth of information about her childhood pain and her most dominant sources of continuing anger and suppressed hurt.

Remember, too, that writing things down makes them more real. Completing this one written exercise can provide volumes of biographic information regarding trauma, and can also provide a sense of which areas to focus on in your recovery.

Once we have an understanding of the relationship of hurt and anger to resentments, the next question is "How do I let go of a resentment?" One answer is to pray for the person toward whom you have a resentment. In my own situation I have done this, but at times have found it very difficult. In those cases, I have found that I can pray for God to relieve me of the resentment.

Another possible solution is to practice acceptance. Life is a struggle, and the sooner we accept this, the easier life becomes. In other words, by accepting that life is sometimes unfair and painful, that things happen to each of us and are sometimes the result of one person's actions, we begin to live in the solution, with our focus on today and not the past. We can be grateful there is a God of Grace to hold onto in our times of trouble.

We should also ask ourselves the question, "Is the person involved in this resentment someone important in my life today?" If the answer is no, then why would you want to have that person take up precious space in your heart and mind that could be filled with loving your family, working on your recovery, or spending quiet time with God?

A long-term resentment can sometimes be based on wrong thinking or a misunderstanding. Years ago, I used to do individual rounds with my addicted inpatients in the presence of their peers. It was powerful in that there was an increased accountability with this method. However, when necessary, I also would do one-on-one rounds, depending on the patient and the nature of his or her issues. There was a man, about sixty-five years old, whom I will call Lester. Lester came to treatment with a huge resentment toward his deceased father. Lester couldn't engage in the treatment process due to the resentment.

In rounds one morning, he told all of us his story. Lester was the oldest of three brothers, and, in many ways, had been the most successful, yet he could never please his father. His father, like himself, was a self-made man and was tough, yet seemed to have a softer side for Lester's brothers but never for him. Lester could never remember his father saying he loved him. He said the final insult came when his father was on his deathbed surrounded by family, and asked everyone to leave but Lester. In his last moments, he reached out his hand to Lester and said, "I'll keep the fires burning for you." After telling this story, Lester looked around the room and said, "Can you believe that his last words were that he would keep the fires of hell burning for me?" I was shocked by Lester's interpretation of his father's statement. I felt his father was saying that he would keep the home fires burning for him, and was making a final attempt to tell his son he loved him and to connect with him alone in that room. When I told Lester that and the majority of people in rounds agreed with me, he wept. His resentment was released, a burden was lifted from him, and he began the journey to recovery.

As I mentioned at the outset of this chapter, unconsciously keeping a resentment may be based purely on having an excuse or reason to continue using alcohol or other drugs. Sometimes just saying this to the addict is enough for him or her to realize this possibility and begin to work more earnestly on the solution found in today, not yesterday.

Another method to resolve resentments is to learn to allow others their sickness. In my treatment of patients, seldom do I use the terms *right, wrong, strong, weak, good,* or *bad.* All imply judgment. I prefer to speak in terms of sickness and health. If a patient can see another person's actions as a reflection of his or her sickness, based, perhaps, on that person's own previous suffering or trauma, it may be easier to let go of the resentment.

Finally, the more spiritually centered a person is, the less room there is for resentments. Working a program of recovery that begins each day with asking for God's presence and companionship fills the heart with blessings, faith, and gratitude, with little room for resentment. Remember, the goal of recovery is peace of mind and serenity, and it is my experience that those can be found only in a spiritual place.

# CHAPTER SIX

# The Power of Addiction

*"Addiction promises immediate gratification,
and all it asks of you is long-term suffering."*

———

*paraphrased from an anonymous
twelve-step reading, "I'm Your Disease"*

The power of addiction is a force built on denial. This power is so dominant in active addiction that addicts can neither see nor hear the devastation and losses occurring around them as a result of their disease. Sometimes, maybe years down the road, some crisis occurs that causes them to "come up for air" and breaks the shell of their denial. They look around and find career, children, time, opportunity, trust of loved ones, physical health, mental health, and, seemingly, God, all gone. While this is an extreme example, unfortunately it is also a fairly common one.

Another scenario is the addict who presents to me in inpatient detoxification. He is at that point in his life and his brain chemistry where he is "using to live and living to use," and none of it feels good anymore.

> **On the front end, the power of addiction is usually based on the substance or behavior doing one or more things for the person that he or she loves, or that nothing else has ever done before.**

As you will find in this book, most of my lectures involve lists. When I lecture on the power of addiction, I have patients raise their hands and individually contribute to the list of what the drug did for them when it felt its best. Typical answers include these:

- Relaxed me

- Gave me energy

- Allowed me to fit in with the crowd

- Gave me courage and self-confidence

- Took away my problems

- Relieved depression

- Gave me a high, euphoria, a rush, etc.

- Made me happy

- Made me feel powerful

- Allowed for intimacy

- Allowed me to sleep

- Made me feel everything more intensely

Despite twenty-plus years of my giving this lecture to probably more than a thousand groups of patients, the list always looks about the same, and almost everyone in each group can identify with almost everything on the list. What does this mean? It could mean that many of our basic human needs are the same, but it certainly means that these individuals all have the same disease of addiction.

This above list is incomplete unless a three-letter word is added at the end of each of the twelve listed items. Can you guess what it is? The answer is the word *now*! None of the "benefits" listed would be of value to the addict unless they happen immediately. Addiction is all about changing the way the one feels *now*. The addict will unconsciously and repeatedly choose immediate gratification at the risk of long-term suffering.

In a Hazelden pamphlet, Tom Cunningham was the first person to coin the term *King Baby* when referring to the spoiled, childlike behavior of the male addict.[1] What a great choice of words. Just like a king at the center of his kingdom, and just like a baby who is in need, the addict will say and do whatever he has to until someone comes to tend to him. So it is with addicts and their need for immediate gratification. By the time patients reach treatment, the addictive behavior is no longer doing what it once did for them—the things on the list above.

As the disease progresses, another list begins to manifest itself. This is a list of negative consequences. Remember, the heart of the definition of addiction is continued use in spite of negative consequences. Some of these negative consequences were mentioned in the first paragraph of this chapter. I would like to comment specifically on a few of these.

One of the most frequent losses patients describe to me is the loss of the trust of their loved ones. Too often patients have the unrealistic expectation that because they enter treatment and are serious about recovery, their spouse or loved ones should trust them in short order. I am continually reminding patients that trust is not lost in a day and will not be regained in a day. One of my favorite sayings in recovery is "I hear the words, but I trust the behavior."

**Recovery is not about just stopping using alcohol and other drugs; it is about demonstrating changed behavior over time, and changed behavior over time is all that loved ones can trust.**

Another negative consequence of addiction is loss of one's identity. The further addicts fall into their addiction, the more all-consuming it becomes. It becomes the center of their world, and, unconsciously, other priorities are pushed to the periphery and eventually lost. The longer the addiction goes untreated, the more it becomes a person's main identity. The addict unconsciously takes on the role of being the victim and/or being bitter about life and tends to blame others for his or her problems. When the denial begins to fade and recovery begins, the addict may find little of his or her old self remaining. This is a scary proposition. In addition, the addict must look at living life on life's terms, and having to become emotionally accountable for him- or herself. This emotional accountability is perhaps one of the toughest hurdles in recovery, and I believe it often results in people choosing repeated relapses over recovery, even to the point of death.

> **Being emotionally accountable has been defined previously in this book, but its crucial role in recovery calls for a restatement of its meaning. Being emotionally accountable for yourself means first no longer blaming others for how you feel or for your lot in life, no longer "needing" problems to perpetuate your addiction, and attempting to identify your most painful feelings and then being willing to risk sharing them with others. For some patients, this means disclosing the long-held secret of sexual abuse. For others, it may be the act of surrender—"jumping off the cliff" and trusting that someone or something will be there to catch you. For others, it may be putting themselves first emotionally for the first time in their lives.**

One other negative consequence I would like to touch upon is the loss of God. The phrase *loss of God* may be a poor choice of words, because I believe He never leaves us. My Higher Power is always standing just outside the door at any moment, day or night. I just have to open the door. But with the disease of addiction, the drug is the power, not God, and the door remains closed. The addict typically operates from a place of self-centeredness in his or her disease. By the time the addict reaches treatment, he or she is not in a good place spiritually; but God, a God of Grace, is still outside the door. As the addict begins the process of recovery, surrender, and acceptance that he or she has a disease, he or she opens the door, and God is there whether that person feels the connection or not.

Two lists—which is more powerful?

| Short-term gain | Long-term pain |
|---|---|
| (What the addictive behavior provided when it felt the best) | (Negative consequences of the addictive behavior) |
| Gave courage | Loss of trust of loved ones |
| Relaxed me | Loss of employment |
| Allowed me to fit into a crowd | Loss of driver's license |
| Felt less inhibited | Loss of children |
| Felt more in control | Loss of marriage |
| Felt more attractive | Loss of significant relationship |
| Allowed for emotional/ sexual intimacy | Loss of freedom |
| Made me funnier | Loss of time and opportunities |
| Allowed me to forget about my problems/took away reality | Loss of mental health |
| Improved sleep | Loss of self-esteem/respect |
| Took away pain | Loss of identity |
| Allowed me to express feelings outwardly | Loss of life |
| Gave me energy | Loss of God/spirituality |

After patients complete the two lists of the lecture (the previous table gives examples of both lists), I often ask them which list is more powerful: the list of when the drug felt best, or the list of negative consequences. The majority of patients respond by saying the list of negative consequences. I then reply, "Well, if that's true, what keeps you using?" For some, the fantasy of what it felt like when it felt its best is still a powerful stimulus for continued use. In fact, we now know that after continued use for a certain length of time, the reward center in the brain is permanently changed.[2]

Next I make a point about denial. I ask the patients when the last time was that they had some hope that using would feel just as good as it did their first time. For most it has been years, and for some many years since the drug felt as good as it first did. Still, they continued to use. That is the power of addiction.

I also point out that in my experience, many patients continue to relapse—not because they aren't looking at the negative consequences of their addiction, but because they refuse to honestly look at how much they loved the drug use when it felt its best and be willing to say good-bye to it anyway.

The following is a copy of an anonymous reading that has been passed around in twelve-step circles for years, called "I'm Your Disease." I think it speaks to the power of addiction.

### I'm Your Disease

I hate meetings. I hate higher power. I hate anyone who has a program. To all who come in contact with me, I wish you death and I wish you suffering.

Allow me to introduce myself. I am the disease of addiction. Cunning, baffling, and powerful, that's me. I have killed millions, and I am pleased. I love to catch you with the element of surprise. I love pretending I am your friend and lover. I have given you comfort, have I not? Wasn't I there when you were lonely? When you wanted to die, didn't you call me? I was there. I love to make you hurt. I love to make you cry. Better yet, I love it when I make you so numb you can neither hurt nor cry. You can't feel anything at all. This is true glory. I will give you instant gratification, and all I ask of you is long-term suffering. I've been there for you always. When things were going right in your life, you invited me. You said you didn't deserve these good things; I was the only one who would agree with you. Together we were able to destroy all things good in your life.

People don't take me seriously. They take strokes seriously, heart attacks seriously, and they even take diabetes seriously. Fools that they are, they don't know that without my help these things would not be made possible.

I am such a hated disease, and yet I do not come uninvited. You choose to have me. So many have chosen me over reality and peace.

More than you hate me, I hate all of you who have a twelve-step program. Your programs, your meetings, your higher power all weaken me, and I can't function in the manner I am accustomed to.

Now I must lie here quietly. You don't see me, but I am growing bigger than ever. When you only exist, I may live. When you live, I only exist. But I am here . . . and until we meet again, I wish you death and suffering.

What has been the most effective way of fighting the power of addiction? The answer, in my opinion, is the twelve-step model of recovery. Since, by the time patients arrive at my inpatient unit, for the majority the first list (of what drugs provided them when they felt the best) no longer applies, I erase this list and ask the thirty or forty patients seated, "Can you recover just by being fully aware of what your addiction has cost you, by looking at the second list?" Most of them sense that the answer is no. What is missing is a way to achieve recovery—a program. Otherwise, one is back to willpower alone, which is ineffective.

The most effective treatment I know is a twelve-step-oriented treatment program. One of the benefits of this form of treatment is that it can give you many of the items on the "immediate gratification" list without your having to pay with all the long-term pain on the "negative consequences" list. The program I teach to patients can improve their self-esteem, help them decrease their fear of people with a new or improved spirituality, and give them a purpose born of being out of self and a peace that comes with working a daily program.

Every addict and everyone working in the field of addiction needs to have a healthy respect for the power of addiction, but also remember that this is a treatable disease. My life has been filled with seeing the blessings of families reunited in recovery, lives restored, and recovering individuals enjoying the best life has to give, one day at a time.

### Chapter Six Notes

1. Tom Cunningham, *King Baby* (Center City, MN: Hazelden Publishing, 1986).

2. National Institute on Drug Abuse. 2010. *Drugs, Brains, and Behavior: The Science of Addiction* [online]. Available from http://www.drugabuse.gov/scienceofaddiction/ (accessed 5 September 2011).

# CHAPTER SEVEN

# Substitute Addictions

*"Why has the will an influence over the tongue
and fingers, not over the heart and liver?"*

———

*—David Hume*

Addiction is a disease with many potential faces, including, but not limited to, alcohol and other drugs. Also, once someone is addicted to alcohol or other drugs— whether he or she is in recovery or not—his or her addiction can generalize to other areas, such as gambling, eating, or sex. When one form of addiction replaces another, it is sometimes referred to as a substitute addiction. It is important to note that all forms of the disease of addiction, whether they involve substances or behaviors, share the same dynamics and characteristics. These characteristics include:

- Compulsion

- Loss of control

- Increased time engaged in addiction at the expense of normal activity

- "Rush," arousal, euphoria, immediate gratification

- Means of "going fast" to relieve emotional pain and stress

- Continued use in spite of negative life consequences

My first introduction to the concept of substitute addiction was at a conference in the mid-1980s. Terrence Gorski, a noted authority on relapse prevention, mentioned these other forms of addiction as relapse triggers for alcohol and other drug addictions. He made the point, as I do with my patients, that where alcohol dependency is concerned, abstinence is only the first step. Recovery is really about changing behavior over time.

Before discussing some of the more studied substitute addictions, it is interesting to first look at terms often used to categorize them. Some people in the field of addiction differentiate between substance addictions related to alcohol and those related to other drugs or to process addictions, such as gambling, Internet, or sexual addiction, which are more behaviorally oriented. Some classify these addictions as being either "positive addictions" (which seems an oxymoron) or "negative addictions." Positive addictions would include workaholism, because work is a positive endeavor; exercise; and Internet addiction, since the Internet serves many productive purposes in our society in terms of communication, business, and technology. On the other hand, addictions to substances and gambling are seen as negative addictions, serving no positive purpose.

Substitute addictions have been the subject of much debate in our society. We live in a culture where the majority of people still see alcohol and other drug addictions and major depression as moral weaknesses and not diseases. In the lectures I give my patients on substitute addictions, I compare all other manifestations of addiction to alcohol and drug dependency. I do not like the terms *process, substance, positive,* or *negative* as defining boundaries for substitute addictions. Instead, I focus on communicating to my patients that with each form of substitute addiction, such as those listed below, the same characteristics as those of drug addiction exist.

**Examples of substitute addictions**
- **Work**
- **Relationships/love**
- **Sex**
- **Gambling**
- **Internet**
- **Food/eating disorders**

When treating patients in the detoxification stage or early stages of recovery, my primary aim with substitute forms of addiction is to convince them that the behavior is the same as that of the active alcoholic or drug addict. With workaholism, for example, the workaholic has the compulsion to work, no matter the consequences. There is a fast pace to it that produces euphoria or a high, and at times a sense of power. Work knows no limits, at the expense of family time, relationships, and even physical health. As with alcohol and other drug addictions, the workaholic is in denial and has little insight into the problems he or she is causing.

Speaking about this reminds me of a young female patient I treated many years ago. She was extremely serious about her recovery and had done everything asked of her in inpatient treatment for her alcohol dependency. She had an excellent discharge plan and relapse prevention plan—with one exception. She was in college at the time and wanted to return to school immediately, which was fine, but she wanted to take eighteen to twenty credit hours, a massive course load. Knowing her to be a perfectionist and somewhat of a workaholic by nature, I tried to convince her that this was not a wise decision. She was certain, however, that she could carry her load at school and fully work her recovery program. Unfortunately, she relapsed, but she quickly returned to treatment, and to my latest knowledge she had solid recovery. She learned two things from this experience: to beware of her workaholism as a relapse trigger, and to accept the limitations that recovery may sometimes place on her.

Many forms of substitute addiction require very specialized treatment. It is also important to note that there are twelve-step support groups specifically for substitute addictions, including gambling, sex, and others.

The remainder of this chapter will discuss my understanding and views on some of the specific substitute forms of addiction. The first is pathologic gambling. Gambling addiction is the only substitute addiction that is listed in the *Diagnostic and Statistical Manual of Mental Health Disorders*.[1] It is listed there as a compulsive disorder. Gambling addicts are often men, under thirty years old, nonwhite, unmarried, and often with less than a high school education. While there are many specialized treatment centers across the country, many of these individuals would be unable to afford treatment. Gambling addicts often begin with a winning streak, but as the addiction progresses, they are no longer gambling to win, whether they realize it or not. They are driven by the adrenaline and the rush of "risking it all," and then are crushed when there is no more money or hope of getting it. In desperation, they sometimes resort to criminal acts to obtain the money to feed their addiction.

For the gambling addict to be interested in a particular form of gambling, three things must be true: (1) the result of the wager must be immediate, (2) the addict must believe intellect is involved in whether he or she wins or loses, and (3) there are no limits on how long he or she can play. With the introduction of video poker came the perfect game for the gambling addict. The number of gambling addicts increased as whole new segments of the population became involved— housewives and college students. For stay-at-home moms, it brought a new kind of excitement and, at first, enjoyment to their lives. For the college student with access to Mom or Dad's credit card and the Internet, the temptation was just too great. He was smart; he knew the odds. It was a way to relieve the boredom of studying, to get a "high," and forget his problems. In the end came too much time on the "net," too much losing, and then failing school and the call from his parents.

Another common substitute addiction is Internet addiction. It is often difficult to diagnose because the addiction may remain hidden and because of the addict's degree of denial. The Internet plays an incredibly important role in our society for business transactions, entertainment, educational programs, and communications. Because of its many applications, it lends itself to a variety of different manifestations of addiction. Some professionals argue that the Internet is primarily a vehicle for preexisting substitute addictions such as gambling, relationship or sexual addiction, or video game addiction. However, the majority of experts would agree that the Internet itself is addictive. Internet addicts may spend thirty to eighty hours a week on the Internet, and go on binges that may last from ten to twenty consecutive hours. As a result, there may be disruption of sleep patterns, increased susceptibility to disease, decreased work performance, worsening home relationships as a result of isolation, and carpal tunnel syndrome (entrapment of the median nerve as it passes through the wrist, causing pain, burning, and numbness in the hand).

Initially, the typical Internet addict was the socially awkward, isolated male who was drawn to the Internet because of the interactive games such as Dungeons and Dragons, where a multitude of players compete with one another, giving the player a fantasy world where he fit in and could achieve a sense of power based on his gaming skills. In addition, with interactive chat rooms, he no longer felt as introverted and could talk more openly while still in the safe surroundings of his room. We know now that Internet addiction affects all ages, genders, and cultural backgrounds, and it is growing.

Relationship addiction or love addiction, terms often used interchangeably, typically can be classified into two types. The first is addiction to being in any relationship at all. With this type, the addict often moves from one relationship to another, seemingly without cause. The second is addiction to a single relationship, often with escalating negative consequences over time if the other person no longer cares for or becomes less interested in the addict. At the core of relationship addiction are poor self-esteem and fear of abandonment. These issues can often be traced to the "don't talk" rule of growing up in an addicted or dysfunctional home where there may have been significant abuse and/or neglect. The relationship addict feels as if he or she will die if not in a relationship. The addict, above all, desires intimacy, but at the same time fears it and flees from it. Relationship addicts also often have a poor sense of their own identity, trust issues, and dependency. More dependent addicts will stay in abusive relationships for the illusion of intimacy, suffering and sacrificing, with little idea of how to be good to themselves. Often seen in drug-addicted relationships, relationship addicts become more and more enmeshed in their situation.

When dealing with either a relationship addict or a sex addict, I sit down with the patient individually and talk about the importance of not engaging in his or her substitute addiction. It is important that there be good communication among staff members about the existence of relationship and/or sexual addiction when it is present in a patient or patients in the community because of the emotional vulnerability of inpatients and the potential for using sex or forming a relationship as a means of relieving stress, defocusing in treatment, and remaining in denial. Moreover, if an adult patient on the unit is a prior victim of sexual abuse, a potential perpetrator may spot his or her vulnerability. With relationship addiction in particular, if a patient returns to treatment after relapsing on alcohol or other drugs, in my experience at least 60 to 70 percent of the time the patient had already begun a relationship while in treatment, started a relationship shortly following treatment, or returned to a toxic past relationship, all against the recommendations of staff while hospitalized. Professionally, I seem much more adept at uncovering previously undisclosed sexual abuse than identifying sexual addiction. Perhaps this is because sexual addiction was not a focus as early on in most psychiatric hospitals.

The literature varies, but it is safe to say that at least 60 percent of sex addicts are victims of sexual abuse, usually in childhood or adolescence. Again, the characteristics given at the beginning of the chapter regarding drug addiction generally apply to the sex addict. Forms of sexual addiction vary greatly. They include compulsive masturbation (one of the earliest forms seen from the standpoint of age), extramarital affairs, one-night stands, obsessive use of pornography, unsafe sex, phone or computer sex, prostitution or use of prostitutes, exhibitionism, obsessive dating through personal ads, voyeurism (watching others) and/or stalking, and sexual harassment. Each of these behaviors must meet all the criteria for addiction to constitute a form of sexual addiction. In my opinion, sex addiction is really not about sex, but about trying to fill that big hole inside created by poor self-esteem and a need for caring and intimacy. While it is true that the sex addict may feel some temporary sense of power where sex is concerned (particularly in contrast to the powerlessness he or she felt as a sexual abuse victim in childhood or adolescence), many addicts feel guilt or shame following the sex.

Sex addicts usually have no insight into why they are acting out sexually. As with other forms of addiction, tolerance develops. With sexual addiction, tolerance is manifested by increased frequency of sex, new conquests, or new or more dangerous types of sexual thrills. The compulsion in the sex addict is to get the feeling of sexual arousal and release. The sex itself is an illusion of intimacy and a means of getting relief from emotional pain and other stressors. As with other forms of addiction, denial plays a major role in the sex addict's thinking. Suicidal thoughts are not uncommon as the negative consequences mount in terms of family, job, health, and so on, in an individual with already poor self-esteem. Guilt, shame, and depression are major issues to be dealt with in treatment.

There are several well-known treatment centers in the country for sexual addiction. Typically the most effective approach is a twelve-step-oriented program and sixty to ninety days of abstinence from sex, best done in a residential setting (although with excellent family, twelve-step, and spiritual support, this can sometimes be accomplished in an outpatient setting). A significant percentage of sex addicts also suffer from drug addiction.[2] Cognitive behavioral therapy may be used to replace addictive thinking with positive recovery thinking. Individual talk therapy is helpful to deal with core issues that may relate to childhood trauma or relationship difficulties, and group therapy is helpful in terms of reducing feelings of isolation and of being different. The group also serves as a powerful means of chipping away at or confronting the addict's denial. Family involvement is critical. Discussion of potential health issues, education about sexual addiction, and family therapy sessions to begin the process of communication and healing are all important, as is aftercare planning for when the patient is discharged.

When discussing gambling addiction, workaholism, Internet addiction, sexual addiction, or relationship addiction, many of the same general therapy modalities hold true, with some exceptions. For instance, with gambling the goal is total abstinence one day at a time with the help of a higher power, but most all of the modalities of therapy are still options. I believe that group therapy, family therapy, talk therapy, and working a twelve-step program are the most critical elements. For workaholism, in the absence of other forms of addiction, individual therapy and family therapy may be most helpful. Certainly, it would be helpful if the workaholic could become much more engaged spiritually and begin his or her day with quiet time, slowing down, and "letting go and letting God."

Relationship addiction therapy closely follows the path of sexual addiction treatment, and you do see overlap between these two manifestations of addiction. Treatment for Internet addiction is difficult because it is often well hidden. Depending on the person's job, abstinence is usually not an option. I have had little experience with Internet addicts, but a review of the literature stresses identifying relapse triggers, reducing use based on a plan made with a mental health professional, and sticking to a certain number of hours on the Internet for things not related to work. This may involve keeping a journal of time or even using a timer when on the Internet. Most important is continued honesty with the mental health professional. Sometimes motivational interviewing is used as a means for addicts to see how their addiction has created negative consequences for the people around them, which may encourage them to get help.

I would like to comment briefly on eating disorders. The three forms of eating disorders are bulimia nervosa, anorexia nervosa, and binge eating disorder. Part of what makes eating disorders so difficult to treat is the frequent coexistence of other psychiatric illnesses such as major depression, obsessive-compulsive disorder, and different personality disorders (for example, borderline personality disorder or avoidant personality disorder)[3]. A variety of different causes have been proposed including AD/HD, genetic factors, peer pressure, idealized body type seen in the media, and early childhood trauma or abuse. I do not feel qualified to treat these patients in my own practice, and would strongly recommend that treating professionals refer patients with this diagnosis to a facility with a history of successful treatment of eating disorders for evaluation or treatment.

After reviewing the phenomenon of substitute addiction in general and then a few of the specific forms it can take in more detail, remember that one can take nearly any activity to the extreme so that it can fit the criteria for substitute addiction in terms of obsessive thinking, compulsive behavior, losing control, and continuing to engage in it despite negative consequences. Over the last few years, when I give lectures to patients in the hospital and talk about relapse or the prospect of discharge and going home, I feel obligated to not only caution them to be aware of the potential for substitute addiction, but to emphasize that we live in an addictive culture. Our country has become a complicated, "going fast," consumer-oriented, pleasure-seeking place. I ask each patient not to follow the crowd, but instead to follow the tools of recovery he or she has been given in treatment. Work a twelve-step model of recovery and remember that commitment, slowing down, struggling, and dealing with emotional pain are all part of living a spiritual life one day at a time.

**Chapter Seven Notes**

1. American Psychiatric Association, *Diagnostic and Statistical Manual of Mental Disorders (DSM-IV)*, Fourth Edition (Arlington, VA: American Psychiatric Publishing, 2000).

2. Patrick Carnes, *Don't Call it Love: Recovery from Sexual Addiction*, (New York: Bantam, 1992).

3. National Institute of Mental Health. 2011. Eating Disorders [online]. Available from http://www.nimh.nih.gov/health/publications/eating-disorders/eating-disorders.pdf (accessed 10 October 2011).

# CHAPTER EIGHT

# Humility

*"Humility, like darkness, reveals the heavenly lights."*
—*Henry David Thoreau*

**H**umility is a term not frequently heard early in the addiction recovery process. However, the longer I work with addicts, the more acutely aware I am that humility is truly at the heart of recovery. I define humility as allowing myself and others our own humanity ("humanness"). I believe that too often in our culture, we only see humility in relation to humbling ourselves, whether it be before God or others, and letting go of our oversized ego or false pride. However, I believe there is so much more to humility.

**Humility is always an
emotionally painful journey.**

Seeing the reality of how we view ourselves from a self-esteem standpoint is often difficult. It has been my experience that the number-one secret of patients in any level of care, whether it be acute inpatient, day treatment (partial hospitalization), intensive outpatient, or group therapy, is a basic feeling of inadequacy—in other words, poor self-esteem. Humility—allowing ourselves to be just one among others—means not only letting go of an increased ego, but also learning to believe that you are just as deserving of having a good life, peace of mind, and the promises that recovery can bring. The following diagram helps to demonstrate this.

↑ Ego

O  O  O  O  O  O _____ Humanity/Humility
O  O  O  O  O  O

↓ Self-esteem

Too often judgment, though unintended, occurs among patients in group. Quick decisions are made about someone based on appearance, speech, body language, or some other aspect of their presentation. This flies in the face of what humility is and what twelve-step recovery is all about. In allowing others their own humanness, we do not judge, we try not to have unspoken expectations, and we attempt to see beyond the outer wrappings of someone's pain and defenses.

I remember first attending a recovery group back in the early 1980s. There was a lady I will call Alice who chaired many of the meetings I attended. She opened each meeting with what seemed to be a plastic smile and a "canned" speech that went something like this: "My name is Alice. I've been coming to these meetings for twenty years. I'm wonderful, it's wonderful; I've had a wonderful day, and it's good to see you!" I listened to this over and over for months, and one evening, after a long day at the hospital seeing a lot of sick patients (I was practicing internal medicine at the time), I came in frustrated and listened to Alice rattle off her speech one more time. Well, I lost it. I leaned across the table, looked at Alice, and said in a menacing voice, "Alice, you say the same thing every week. This program is about change. When are you going to change anything?" My doing that was against every principle of recovery. Alice slowly leaned across the table, looked me in the eyes, and said, "Jim, don't tell me what I've changed unless you've walked in my shoes." That was one of my first lessons in humility, and after that, Alice began to share some of her childhood trauma of growing up in an alcoholic home and the changes she had made since joining a family recovery program. In turn, I talked about my own fears in childhood and always feeling like an imposter.

Another story relating to humility that comes to mind concerns my former pastor, Steve, at a Baptist church years ago. At the time my wife sang in the choir. She approached Steve after he had finished his sermon one Sunday and asked him to attend a recovery meeting with her. Being in recovery, she had watched Steve's message change over the months to be more and more about a God of Grace. Not being an alcoholic, Steve asked why. Virginia said she thought he would like what he would find there.

After attending one of these meetings, Steve's first comment was "I am amazed at the amount of humility in that meeting. Sometimes we need more of that in church." The preacher understood that in the recovery meeting, no one was giving advice or judging anyone. Everyone seemed genuinely glad that everyone else was there, and people openly shared their experiences, both of their active addiction and of their journeys to recovery. There seemed to be an atmosphere of acceptance and spirituality within those walls.

**Remember, the goal of recovery is serenity and peace of mind, and it is the road of humility that leads to this place.**

One of my favorite poems is entitled "If" by Rudyard Kipling. It is about a boy's journey to manhood, but to me what Kipling so eloquently describes is really the essence of humility, as the following excerpt demonstrates:

*If you can dream—and not make dreams your*
    *master;*
*If you can think—and not make thoughts your*
    *aim;*
*If you can meet with Triumph and Disaster*
*And treat these two impostors just the same;*
*If you can bear to hear the truth you've spoken*

*Twisted by knaves to make a trap for fools,*
*Or watch the things you gave your life to, broken,*
*And stoop and build 'em up with worn-out tools;*

It is impossible to separate humility from spirituality. The idea of being out of self, being one among others, not being judgmental, and finding peace and serenity from a single power source—in my case, a God of my understanding, a God of Grace—makes perfect sense.

Until the addict is willing to surrender to God's will, humility is not possible. The repeated disasters, embarrassments, and defeats of the addict's life will painfully run on self-will and eventually lead him or her to a first sense of humility. In lectures, I often talk about the necessity of going through the fear that occurs when, on their first day in inpatient treatment, addicts move from a place of self-will (going fast in their addiction) to being asked to stop and be still. It is that kind of emotional pain that envelops the addict on her or his journey to humility. While addicts must attain this humility to some degree to achieve recovery, reaching this point is not the end, but only the beginning where humility is concerned.

**The humility I experience today is**
**something I embrace and own as part**
**of God within me. It is a true source of**
**serenity when I am most in touch with it.**
**It is something to be desired even when,**
**at times, reaching it is painful.**

Another aspect of humility that is critically important to recovery is becoming a good listener. The person with "all the answers" has no need to listen and also lacks humility, while the person with humility sees him- or herself as one among others and capable of gaining insight and knowledge from each new encounter. Some indicators of a poor listener are interrupting your sentence or finishing it for you. The mark of a good listener is someone who sits quietly, hears everything that is said, and, when you have finished speaking, responds by saying something along the lines of "I hear you."

Only by being a good listener can we be open to learning. Learning to be a good listener is synonymous with being open-minded. Recovery means learning a way of living that is the opposite of addictive thinking and behavior.

Too often, humility is given little attention in our society and is greatly misunderstood. Living in a world based on production and performance as a measure of material success, too many people see humility as reflecting poor self-esteem and self-deprecation. Who wants that? But in my opinion, humility is just what people in our fast-paced, consumer-oriented world need the most.

To me, a person with humility is someone who is comfortable with him- or herself, his or her shortcomings and talents—someone who is able to be out of self, be nonjudgmental, and see the "specialness" in others. I make it a point to tell patients that they will seldom hear me use the words *right, wrong, strong, weak, good,* or *bad* because they all imply judgment in relation to others or the disease of addiction. In the spiritual sense, I gladly acknowledge my weakness and God's amazing strength, power, and grace. By my acceptance of this, I truly experience humility. Humility is the acceptance of ourselves just as we are, with all our imperfections, and genuinely smiling at that. The smile comes when we remember to see ourselves as God sees us—as His children, radiant in His perfect light and resting in His loving arms as a result of our trust and faith. Grace is ever-present as a reminder of God's unfailing love, forgiveness, and acceptance.

One final aspect of humility that needs further discussion is *how God can use our brokenness to help others*. As I have learned and continue to learn as God uses my weakness, trials, and suffering to help others, this can only happen when I make enough time for Him in my life. It is through trusting in God and His spirit within us that we are given strength for the coming day and the patience to look for His purpose. For me, humility is the ultimate path to peace.

# CHAPTER NINE

# Expectations and Acceptance

*"The first step toward change is
awareness. The second is acceptance."*

—
—*Nathaniel Branden*

In my work with addicts and their families, unspoken and unrealistic expectations seemed to be the rule, not the exception. One of my earliest lectures was on expectations and acceptance. Since my philosophy of treating addiction is to talk about issues in terms of healthy and unhealthy, because addiction is an illness, I divide expectations into two categories:

1.  **Healthy expectations, which are spoken and realistic**

2.  **Unhealthy expectations, which are unspoken and/or unrealistic**

During my lecture I first ask my patients to define expectations. Usually they find it difficult to put into words. The best and simplest working definition is to say that an expectation is "what I would like to see happen in a given situation or from a given person or persons." An expectation is not a demand. This fact is crucial to communication in couples therapy. For instance, when you express a healthy expectation that is realistic and spoken, you cannot control the other person's response, but you know you have communicated in a healthy way to your partner. An example of communicating a healthy expectation from me to one of my patients would be "I have the expectation that you are in lecture at 10:30 a.m. and that you bring a pen and pad with you to take notes if needed." An example of an alcoholic in recovery returning home and communicating a healthy expectation to a brother who is a drinker would be "I have the expectation that you will not bring alcohol into my house or come to my house intoxicated." This may be hard, but it is setting a healthy boundary.

Most of our expectations as human beings involve unhealthy expectations, and I'm not just talking about addicts. How many of us will make a statement after some unspoken expectation is unmet, such as "If you really love me, I shouldn't have to tell you," or "You should know how I feel"? I believe that more than 90 percent of our daily expectations are unspoken. We wake up with expectations of the weather, the traffic, the number of problems the day will bring, our boss's mood, whether our friend will remember to call, or whether our spouse will check on us during the day. And with each of these unspoken expectations, we set ourselves up to be potentially more fearful, hurt, or angry. Much of the time we are unaware of these unspoken expectations that complicate our lives.

Now let's take a closer look at unrealistic expectations. If I am someone who tries to always be in control and unconsciously expects others to live by the same rules as I do, that is an unrealistic expectation. No one is exactly like me, can read my thoughts, or has had my life experiences, even for a given day; therefore, no one will behave or speak exactly as I do. Let's take another example. If I am someone who expects perfection from my employees, then that is unrealistic, and a breeding ground for resentment, conflict, hurt, and anger.

These examples are more general scenarios. Now consider the addicted family that is dealing with a progressive, potentially fatal illness. First, let's look at the addict who is in his or her active disease and in denial about his or her addictive thinking. At the heart of that thinking is the need for problems. As long as there is a problem, there is a reason or excuse to use. Also central to addictive thinking is the need to externalize problems, that is, to blame others for what is wrong in the addict's life. With these two facts in mind, let's see how unhealthy expectations fit into addictive thinking. First, when someone has unspoken expectations, others are always falling short of the mark, and this allows the addict a continuing, unlimited source of resentments, problems, and reasons to remain in conflict, blame others, and continue to use. Secondly, since another aspect of addictive thinking is a self-centered view of the world, much of the addict's thinking, including his or her expectations, is unrealistic, and again provides fertile ground for conflict, resentments, hurt, and fear. Remember, in the midst of active addiction, the addict will cling to the role of victim or of being bitter about life with little insight.

One of the more common examples of unrealistic expectations for an addict is when he (let's call him Will) is in twelve-step treatment for ten days and, during that time, breaks through much of his denial and painfully surrenders to being powerless over alcohol and other drugs. He begins to work earnestly in a one-day-at-a-time program in treatment and is given positive feedback by the staff and his peers. He decides to call his wife Jenny and tell her about his progress.

When Jenny answers the phone, Will says, "Hi, it's me. I just wanted to call and tell you what's happened. Since I've been here, I've cried more than I have in ten years. I've admitted I'm an addict, and I know now I have a disease and I'm powerless. I'm so sorry for all the things I've said and done to you and the kids. I would do anything to take it all back, but I promise things are going to be different." There is a pause on the other end of the line. Then Jenny says, "I don't trust you," and hangs up. What is Will's unrealistic expectation? It is that just because he knows he has experienced a profound breakthrough toward entering recovery, his wife will believe him and trust him. I wonder how many times Jenny has heard Will make promises and then be unable to keep them in the past.

I have to remind my patients constantly that trust isn't lost in a day, and it certainly won't be gained back in a day.

This is difficult for the addict because impatience is a primary characteristic of his or her disease.

**The only thing that Jenny, like any other family member, will be able to trust is changed behavior over time.**

Unhealthy expectations also play a major role for the family members of the addict. I believe unrealistic expectations are so common because many family members, at least initially, see addiction as a moral weakness and not as an illness. Therefore, expectations such as "if you just love your wife and children enough you'll quit" are only natural. The problem with this is that it implies that willpower is the solution. Addiction is a disease, and no disease can be managed successfully with willpower alone. Therefore, this is an unrealistic expectation.

Another unrealistic expectation is that addicts can successfully control or cut back on their behavior so that it doesn't cause problems. By definition, addiction means continued use despite negative consequences; therefore, this, too, is an unrealistic expectation. The addict will often relapse because of the unrealistic expectation that his or her family will understand that he or she has a disease. I remind patients that family members are surrounded by a society that generally sees addiction as a moral weakness, and that all it takes to quit is to try harder. Also, the family often has not had the benefit of the education and treatment that the patient has received. Finally, I caution the patient that his or her addictive thinking may be the real underlying problem. It's in these times of confusion, fear, denial, blame, and resentment that I make two things very clear:

- To the addict, I say, "No one person or one thing is so powerful that it can make you take a drink or use."

- To the family member, I say, "You are not so powerful that any one thing you say or do will make the addict drink or use."

Finally, let me mention the children in an addicted home. They learn not to talk about what goes on in the home. They learn by their experience not to trust, and with that comes a marked decrease in expectations of others. They learn not to feel as a way to cope day to day. Through certain roles, they unconsciously attempt to be safe and get some needs met. Whatever expectations they do have are certainly limited by the family disease of addiction.

Since the beginning of this chapter, I have talked primarily about unhealthy expectations as they relate to people in general and to those struggling with addiction in particular. Having said all that, I now want to state that for all of us, and especially for the addict, *a major tool of recovery is to try to have no expectations of others.* Keep in mind that the goal of recovery from addiction is to have peace of mind or serenity. Common sense says that the fewer expectations we have of others or of situations today, the more likely we are to be at peace. Also, in terms of addiction, unhealthy expectations feed addictive thinking and behavior. Therefore, letting go of expectations reinforces recovery.

Additionally, when I have a lot of expectations, my focus is on others. In recovery, my focus needs to be on myself, for

I am the only one I can change, or, as they say in recovery meetings, "If I'm not the problem, there is no solution."

If I have no expectations, when something good happens I can be just as grateful, but when something bad happens, I haven't set myself up to be disappointed, hurt, fearful, or angry. Trying to have no expectations of others is closely aligned with humility because it involves letting go of the need to judge other people. Somehow I don't think having a lot of expectations fits well with the twelve-step concepts of slowing down and simplifying your life.

Before leaving the subject of expectations, one further question needs to be explored: where do our expectations, in general, originate from? I believe the answer lies in our upbringing, our philosophy of life, and our rules for living, including our culture biases. When I ask patients to try to have no expectations, I realize I am asking them in a sense to change or question many of their rules for living. As I begin to examine some of the rules, I see that to change them almost invariably involves one key element—acceptance— which initially can be quite painful.

Let's look at the following list of rules that set people up for unhealthy expectations, and explore new rules for each based on acceptance.

1. **Life ought to be fair.** Many of us know in our heads that life is not fair, but it doesn't mean that's how we react emotionally. We do someone a kindness, expecting at least a thank you, and instead we get anger in return. We see tragic things happen to innocent people and become bitter. While the examples and

explanation of this first rule could take up an entire page, let me just say this: from a spiritual standpoint, I don't believe that everything that happens is God's will. Does He have the power to intervene? I believe God does have a plan ultimately for each of us if we follow His path. He doesn't expect perfection. He expects us to wander from the path even when we find it and to have trust and faith in Him. God expects us to struggle as part of living in a broken world, but at the same time, the more time we spend with Him, the more we find peace in the midst of the struggles. In this world we not only pay for our poor choices sometimes, but we suffer from the cruelty and sickness of others. We cannot know what God's ultimate plan is for each one of us, but if we seek to be near Him and spend time with Him, we will know the full measure of His limitless love and grace.

We live in a world full of stress, serious problems, and frequent tragedy. Each of us has had calamity in our life, but asking "Why me?" is not the answer. Having enough trust and faith that there is a power greater than us who can help us through the storm is the answer. Therefore, the new rule to replace "Life ought to be fair" that practices acceptance is "Life is a struggle, and the sooner we accept it, the easier life becomes."

Addicts, as well as many others, believe that being in control is how to achieve success and happiness in life. People who follow this rule use it as a survival skill, usually having learned it in childhood. As long as they make the rules, no one can back them into a corner with their feelings. People like this often are very uncomfortable with change. Acceptance for people with this issue means accepting that they can only change themselves, not others. A lot of work in treatment is centered upon identifying one-word core feelings and then taking the risk of expressing them in group process without further explanation. This usually means talking less, and working on becoming a good listener.

2.  **Being right is very important.** This rule for living is similar to the previous one. Often I find that people's need to be right is just a poor excuse for injured self-esteem. People usually don't show this feeling of inadequacy or poor self-worth outwardly, and it is sometimes hidden beneath an oversized ego. Unconsciously, these people decide, "Well, at least if I'm right that means something," and, like the controlling person, make the rules so no one can back them into a corner with their feelings.

**Being right often becomes increasingly important if someone doesn't feel good about him- or herself.**

Unfortunately, the need to always be right puts one in constant conflict, particularly with the people he or she loves the most. Where acceptance is needed here is to accept that being right is not important when weighed against the conflict and emotional pain it causes. Letting go of being right also creates an openness that can allow suppressed feelings to surface. It is necessary to risk exposing feelings of inadequacy and experiences of past trauma in order to find peace.

3.  **Other people's approval is important to my self-worth.** In my experience, this is a recipe for continued worsening of already-struggling self-esteem. The need for someone to seek approval to feel better about him- or herself implies feeling uncomfortable without that approval, and it seems logical that, consciously or unconsciously, a person will present him- or herself to others in ways that are intended to please that individual. In doing so, the person may lose more of his or her own sense of self, which is so precious and special. No one will obtain everyone's approval, because

people have their own baggage and agendas and may approve or disapprove based on their own attitudes and feelings. Thus, hoping for everyone's approval is a completely unrealistic expectation.

**Acceptance lies in remembering that our self-worth comes from within, from our special gifts, from our being a child of God, and from understanding humility—that we are just as deserving as anyone of the blessings of this world.**

While the above represent only a few rules for living that I frequently see that set the addict or family member up for unhealthy expectations, I hope that by these examples you can begin to see how in the midst of a crisis, such as active addiction, it is important to examine our old rules for living and replace those that are unhealthy with new rules that allow us to be good to ourselves and others. In doing this, we first look at unhealthy expectations and their destructive influences. Then we draw the conclusion that trying to have no expectations, one day at a time, is a wonderful tool of recovery. Finally, we determine that in order to rid ourselves of many of our unhealthy expectations, we have to look at some of our old rules for living that foster those expectations. Once we examine them, we find that acceptance is the painful key to letting go of these rules, making progress in recovery, and finding peace of mind.

There is one area of acceptance that needs mentioning that is directly related to relapse: not accepting the limitations that the disease of addiction places on someone. It is difficult for individuals who are new in recovery to accept that attending recovery meetings has to be the first priority, and other activities, for the most part, must take a backseat. Addicts also often have difficulty accepting that they can't treat physical pain the exact same way that someone without a history of drug addiction can. The limitation of needing to avoid surroundings that are potential relapse triggers for addiction is also difficult.

One final area of acceptance is to realize how small our world really is. I demonstrate this point with patients in lecture sometimes by making the rather confusing and somewhat callous-sounding statement to them, "I care about every one of you, but none of you are important in my life." I then go on to explain that my world in a lot of ways is as small as the world of those who would be there to mourn my passing if I died tomorrow. I give the example that if I were to drive to the hospital tomorrow and be killed in an automobile accident, some of my patients might be very saddened by that news, but it wouldn't keep them from continuing with their treatment or eating their meals. The point that I am trying to make is that it is so important in early recovery and in life to have our priorities in line and not forget those relationships that are most dear to us.

That does not mean that from a spiritual standpoint you shouldn't be open each day to caring about each person you meet and work on trying to be an example of true humility.

I hope that from this chapter you can see the important and intertwined relationship between expectations and acceptance, and their significance to recovery from addiction.

# CHAPTER TEN

# Daily Tools of Recovery

*"The best thing about the future is that
it comes only one day at a time."*

*—Abraham Lincoln*

This chapter is somewhat of a compilation of several other chapters, with additional helpful suggestions as to how to get from waking up in the morning to going to bed at night without an addictive substance and with as much serenity as possible. When I give this lecture, I ask the audience to make a poster of the following list and place it either next to their bed, on the refrigerator, or somewhere else where it will be seen daily. In the following items listed, you will notice some repetition since the majority of these subjects have been discussed in previous chapters, but it is important to present them in this context.

1.  **Set aside a morning quiet time.** This is
    probably the most crucial of the daily tools. It
    means getting up early enough each morning
    to sit down and consciously say to yourself,
    "This is my quiet time and a commitment to
    my recovery today." Remember, if you take
    the action, the feelings will follow. Then—if
    you have any comfort with the idea of a higher
    power or God—say a prayer. Next, just be still
    for five minutes and try to clear your mind of
    worry, fear, or other thoughts. This will be
    difficult at first if you are new in treatment or
    are not accustomed to making time for silence,
    peace, and God. At the end of this time, find a
    specific focus for the day.

    Recovery is an "inside job." Look inside yourself
    and ask the question, "What's my stuff?" Are you
    a caretaker, an attention seeker, a perfectionist,
    a controller, someone quick to anger, someone
    who is silent and lost, a comedian, a liar even
    when it would be easier to tell the truth, or
    someone who is immensely arrogant? Whatever
    your "stuff" is—and believe me, we all have
    it—choose one thing to work on today that will
    make a positive change in you and increase the
    likelihood of recovery. If you are a compulsive
    liar, then concentrate on honesty. If you are
    silent and lost, then speak up at least once today.
    If you follow these simple directions for quiet
    time in the first five to ten minutes of your day,

you may start to notice a difference in yourself in only a matter of a few such mornings.

2. **Take the hard choice.** You don't have to know anything about twelve-step recovery to use this tool; it applies to everyone. When you are faced with a choice, take the hard choice, and ninety-nine out of one hundred times it will be both the sober choice and the healthy choice. When it comes to addiction, what comes naturally for the addict is his or her sickness— the easy choice. The recovery-supportive choice is always difficult. It should be noted that the easy choice also comes more naturally to people in general; however, addicts are especially vulnerable to it. For a given characteristic, such as how we deal with anger, we tend to gravitate toward one end of the spectrum or the other. We either tend to be too reactive or tend to repress our anger. In either case, the hard choice is to seek the middle ground.

   With this tool of recovery, I feel I always need to remind new addicts in treatment that, in actuality, they should be making as few choices as possible since, when it comes to their addiction, they are the last people to know what is best for them.

3. **Learn to be in the moment.** There have been a number of books written about this subject, that is, one's ability to be "in the now." How this

relates to recovery from addiction and life's daily challenges begins with the fact that we all have times during certain days or whole days when we struggle emotionally. Even the person working a spiritually based, one-day-at-a-time recovery program is going to have days when he or she is filled with fear or resentment. In these times, what is most important is to get to bedtime that evening without drinking or using, and with as much serenity as possible. Being in the moment helps with this. If you can get involved in some activity for an hour or two, and during that time you "forget about" your fear or resentment, then that is a blessing and a valid tool of recovery. The activity may range from talking with a friend to playing cards, to working on business, to working out, to digging in the garden. It will be different for different people.

4. **Try to have no expectations of others, especially family.** A previous chapter was devoted to expectations and acceptance. Let me summarize by saying that by having no expectations, we can be just as grateful when good things happen, and yet if there is a bad result, we do not set ourselves up to be more disappointed, hurt, or angry. Typically, most of our expectations are unhealthy, unspoken, and/or unrealistic, and this contributes to the escalating conflict in the addicted home and in relationships overall. Furthermore, when we

have no expectations of others we are much less likely to judge them and more likely to be at peace with ourselves, and to recognize that we are the only ones we can change.

5.  **Understand the relationship between hurt and anger.** The subject of hurt versus anger has been touched on in various chapters in this book. Remember, as children we learn unconsciously that it is either not okay to be hurt or not okay to be angry, and we develop an internal switch such that if anger is not okay, that switch is flipped and anger is either never expressed or is outwardly expressed as hurt. This basic understanding of the relationship of hurt to anger touches on so many aspects that are critical to recovery from addiction and to living in a broken world.

    The main thing to recognize as a tool of recovery is that if you have an easier time expressing anger outwardly to others than hurt, then one of your main focuses in recovery should be on bringing to the surface and expressing your repressed hurt. This may be extremely difficult and at times frightening, but with help, it is freeing and crucial to your peace of mind. In the opposite vein, if you have an easier time expressing hurt outwardly to others than anger, it is your repressed anger that needs to be the primary focus. It may require the help of a

therapist, psychologist, or other professional
to do this, but it is well worth the effort. One
simple way of beginning this process is to do this
exercise: if anger comes easiest, the next time
you become angry, take a step back afterward
and ask yourself, "What was going on there that
I might have been hurting about?" If you express
hurt most frequently, do just the opposite.

6. **Attend twelve-step meetings, get and use a
sponsor, and read twelve-step literature.** This
tool of recovery applies to all addicts, regardless
of substance(s) or behaviors. To enter recovery
and to maintain it, you must work a daily
program, and part of that daily program includes
attendance at recovery meetings, sponsor
contact, and reading twelve-step literature.
Why is it so important to do these three things?
One of my wife's favorite sayings in recovery
addresses this very concisely: "You can't store
awareness."

Early in the recovery process, addicts need to
put themselves in places where they will hear
and observe recovery-oriented thinking and
behavior as often as they can. That is why people
recommend going to ninety meetings in the
first ninety days of recovery. Since the addict is
the last person to know what is best for him or
her, listening in meetings and taking questions
and problems to a sponsor results in getting

recovery-oriented answers. Also, twelve-step meetings are often the place where people feel truly accepted, can leave the troubles of the world outside those doors for an hour, and find some peace. Finally, recovery-oriented thinking is the opposite of addictive thinking; therefore, the more we place ourselves in situations where we hear or read recovery-oriented thoughts, the better it is for us.

7. **Practice communication skills. "I have a problem"—talk to a third person.** It is sad how the first few words we choose can have such a drastic effect on the rest of a conversation. Let's assume something has happened between two friends, and one of them is feeling angry. What happens too often is that one person confronts the other and says something like "You made me so angry when you avoided me at the meeting this morning." This immediately puts the other person on the defensive, and tells him that he is responsible for the first person's anger. It also makes one wonder what the first person's motive was in making the statement.

Having considered this scenario as an example, let's explore a healthier way of communicating in the same situation.

The person feeling angry should talk about it with someone who can be objective, a good listener whose judgment he or she trusts. In this way, the anger may be resolved without ever meeting one-on-one with the friend. If this doesn't work, I suggest giving things time and prayer, or talking with someone else. Then, and only then, if the person feels the need to speak with the friend, he or she needs to look at his or her motive. Too often a person's motive is not healthy. The motive may be to change the other person, to be right, to hurt the other person, or to exact an apology.

**The only truly healthy motive is to express your feelings, because your feelings matter, with no expectation of a result.**

The healthy way to approach the friend in the above situation would be to ask if you could speak to him or her for a moment. Then begin by saying, "I'm having a problem. It's my problem. Since yesterday at the meeting, I have felt angry. I thought you avoided me, and I reacted negatively. I just wanted you to know, if I appeared angry, what's going on with me." In this way, there is no argument, and you are taking ownership of your own feelings.

8. **Review your day.** Just as you began your day, at the end of the day sit somewhere quietly by

yourself and review your day, asking yourself,
"Did I do what I could do for my recovery today?"
Do not expect perfection, only progress. For
example, did you have daily quiet time? Did
you have a focus for the day? Did you make a
recovery meeting? If you did these things and
basically feel good about working your program
today, then pat yourself on the back, because you
did not only the most loving thing for yourself,
but also the most loving thing for everyone
you love and who cares about you. If you didn't
do a good job with your program today, but
didn't drink or use, then be grateful and make a
commitment to do a better job tomorrow, one
day at a time.

## DAILY TOOLS OF RECOVERY

1. Set aside a morning quiet time.
2. Take the hard choice.
3. Learn to be in the moment.
4. Try to have no expectations of others, especially of family.
5. Understand the relationship between hurt and anger.
6. Attend twelve-step meetings, get and use a sponsor, and read twelve-step literature.
7. Practice communication skills.
8. Review your day.

# CHAPTER ELEVEN

# Spirituality

*"There, but for the grace of God, go I."*

—*John Bradford*

**W**hile this is not the last chapter in the book, it is the chapter that I wrote last. One reason is that writing it was so personal, and I want so much for it to communicate clearly both my own feelings on spirituality and a form of spirituality that for many will open a doorway into an emotionally safe and loving spiritual relationship. In terms of addiction, using the word "God" is probably too specific. For addicts or for people in general who struggle with the concept of God, my hope is that by accepting that they are powerless over addiction or that they are in such great emotional pain that it is impossible to make good decisions, they will look for a power source outside themselves to help guide them in their recovery. Finally, I wish to say that writing this chapter was a humbling experience.

> **Today, I view spirituality as a person's one-to-one relationship with a power greater than him- or herself—in my own case, a God of Grace.**

In relation to treatment, I see spirituality as the key element in the twelve-step model of recovery. An excerpt from a recent book entitled *Addiction and Spirituality* states that "the essence of spirituality is grounded in relationship with God and the expression of spirituality is experienced in community."[1] This mirrors the concept of working an individual daily spiritual program of recovery, but attending daily meetings (community) to experience spiritual fellowship.

In Chapter Eight ("Humility") this connection to spirituality was briefly mentioned, but I would like to explore it in more depth. Typically, we talk about recovery from addiction and other illnesses involving the body, spirit, and mind. I believe humility is a sturdy, wide bridge that connects the mind and spirit. In addiction hospitals, following detoxification, the majority of the remaining time in treatment centers like ours is spent on the mental or emotional aspects of recovery. Issues that often surface include low self-esteem, increased ego, judgment of others, caretaking, selfishness, the need to be in control, and childhood abuse, among others. I have found that in dealing with these painful subjects, understanding and utilizing humility is critically important.

Earlier, humility was described as allowing ourselves and others "humanness," that is, accepting that being human means we all make mistakes, we all are special in our own way, and no one is better than anyone else. Most importantly, we are all children of God, and He loves us all. Using humility as a way of approaching and dealing with emotional pain offers a means of change that can provide relief for people spiritually, emotionally, and physically. For many of the serious emotional issues listed above, fear is the underlying core feeling—and it is trust and faith that can relieve that fear.

As with any work in treatment, working on humility is painful. Letting go of an increased ego and letting others see the insecurities beneath it is frightening, but inevitably people will reach out to you in your pain, embrace you, and admire your courage for risking. Following this painful risking comes relief, and with relief, peace of mind.

**Spirituality is a process, as is recovery.**

Remember that the goal of recovery is peace of mind and serenity, and peace is the gift God gave us and desires for us. When patients first come into inpatient treatment, they are often exposed for the first time to this concept of spirituality. Too often, they think that to have a successful treatment or a chance of recovery they must have a clear, special connection to God or a higher power. I am quick to point out to my patients that spirituality is a process, as is recovery. It truly gives patients a sense of relief that there is no expectation by anyone that they be in a certain place spiritually by a certain time, and to know they have the freedom to work a daily recovery program without a particular timetable. Something else that is definitely true, but hard to communicate in words, is that I often see God at work in patients before they recognize the spirituality already present within them.

I also remind patients that in their active addiction, by the nature of this disease of denial, everything was pushed from sight, including God. Therefore, it is usually impossible for them to be in a good place spiritually when they arrive in treatment. In fact, in twelve-step meetings people often share how their active addiction left them "spiritually bankrupt." This doesn't mean a lack of faith or belief in God, necessarily. It may only signify that they either had lost faith or had forgotten to open the door to let God in each day. To reconnect requires action. Prayer may seem awkward at first, but if you keep taking action, the feelings will follow. A wonderful connection will be reestablished or established for the first time when you realize there is something greater at work in your life that can be a source of comfort even in the midst of turmoil.

Over the years, I have seen so many "God-incidences." I used to call them coincidences, until I obtained spirituality in my life. If you approach each day with a positive spiritual attitude, you will find God-incidences, too. As an example, a man, unknown to me at the time, was in the midst of a severe depression. He had called a person he knew in recovery who gave him my wife's number. She listened to him and said, "You need to talk to Jim." As I listened to him, his depression was so much like my own when it began many years ago. I knew how he was feeling before he could tell me. I explained to him that he was in the midst of a major depression and needed medication and therapy. At the time he didn't know me, but he trusted what I said. Following that, I saw him in therapy weekly for over a year. Long after, he was no longer a patient of mine; he became a lifelong friend and has been an inspiration for this chapter on spirituality.

**There is something spiritual in this collective silence, as if God is there walking among us and being within us in our pain.**

Spirituality can come in many forms. One way I believe it manifests itself is as follows: Sometimes, when I have finished giving a lecture that is very emotional, there is a "heavy" silence in the room. After a minute or two, I will often ask patients what they think that silence means. The answer is usually that most of the people in the room are dealing individually with their own painful memories or feelings. To me, there is something spiritual in this collective silence, as if God is there walking among us and being within us in our pain. I thank God for those moments because I believe the more of that heavy silence a patient is exposed to, the better his or her chances for recovery.

When I first started working in the field of addiction medicine in the mid-1980s, alcohol and drug addiction treatment centers were almost exclusively twelve-step oriented, and psychiatry had little or nothing to do with twelve-step recovery. This was easily seen at conferences, such as SECAD in the early 1990s. We had to be very careful with selection of speakers and topics so as not to offend or detract from the integrity of twelve-step treatment. Much has changed since those days. Now, co-occurring disorders (addiction and mental illness) programs are the norm, not the exception. These patients have two diagnoses: one psychiatric and the other substance related.

Now, through research, we talk much more in terms of addiction as a disease of the brain, using PET scans to demonstrate the destructive nature of methamphetamines and other drugs. A recent article by Dr. Marc Galanter, "Evidence-Based Medicine and Spirituality," which appeared in *The American Journal of Psychiatry*, noted an association between serotonergic activity and inclination toward spirituality.[2] This is important since the neurotransmitter serotonin plays such a vital role both in mood disorders, such as major depression, and in addiction.

The success of twelve-step meetings has raised some important questions for contemporary psychiatry. A Project MATCH study done on twelve-step meetings showed that scores on spirituality in recovering alcoholics at three years were predictive of positive outcomes at ten years. Of patients who attended twelve-step meetings, those who reported a spiritual awakening were three times more likely to be abstinent three years later than those who did not. In this latter group, greater religiosity had no effect on outcome.[3]

In dealing with spirituality, the subject of religion is always close at hand. In a pilot study in the *Journal of Religion and Health*, definitions and evaluations of religion and spirituality were explored. Content analysis of definitions reveals religion as objective, external, and ritual or organizational practices that one performs in a group setting and that guide one's behavior. Spirituality is defined as internal, subjective, and divine experience or direct relationship with God.[4]

Spirituality is acquiring more and more attention in the medical field as we try to fill the gaps that have existed for so long in treating the whole patient. Attention to spirituality is now a prerequisite by the Joint Commission on Accreditation of Healthcare Organizations. It has to be included in a psychiatric assessment. It is also a subject of much debate in the training of nurses in intensive care areas. Finally, it has recently been added to the training requirements for psychiatric residencies.

I associate spirituality with quiet time. In contrast, there is a certain "going fast" that accompanies the active disease of addiction that doesn't allow for quiet time. More significantly, as someone becomes consumed in his or her addiction, it becomes the center of his or her world. Every day he or she is obsessed with obtaining, using, manipulating, and so on. By the time the addict gets to treatment, he or she is empty, used up, exhausted, physically miserable, and frightened. It is only by going from this place of going nonstop in the insanity of addiction, and working through the fear of slowing down and doing things someone else's way, that he or she can become spiritually connected. To do this is extremely difficult because by nature addicts are impatient and deny their feelings. Now the addict is being asked to be still and trust a spiritual process.

As I described in Chapter Ten, one of the most important coping skills that I teach my patients is to have morning quiet time. From a spiritual standpoint, the amount of time spent alone in communication with God is directly related to a person's peace of mind. To accomplish this peace of mind, the addicts in early recovery must adhere to the structure of morning quiet time, and gradually, over weeks to months, increase the amount of time.

I ask them each morning to get up at least ten minutes earlier than they planned and to sit down in a chair or at a table. First, they are to say a prayer if they have any belief in a higher power or God. I tell them not to worry if they are uncomfortable. *Prayer, like everything else, takes practice.* Then I ask them to try to clear their minds and be still for five minutes. If they wish to read a daily reading related to recovery, that is fine. Then, at the end of five minutes, I ask each of them to find a focus for the day. The focus should be something specific about him- or herself. It should be a quality or behavior that by working on or changing it, it will increase the likelihood of sustaining recovery. For instance, if someone is a constant worrier, he might choose a focus of turning things over to God. If someone is a constant talker, her focus would be to talk less and become a better listener. By setting aside these first ten minutes of the day, a person is putting both spirituality and recovery first.

Often as discharge approaches, a patient will state that he or she plans to attend only church and not twelve-step meetings. My response is that I would like him or her to do both, since I believe there are gifts each can give that the other cannot. The fear I have—and I will voice this to patients when appropriate—is that some churches by doctrine or leadership may tend to be judgmental and fail to remember that addiction is an illness, and that it only adds further stigma for addicts when they moralize a disease.

Finally, let me speak about the God of my understanding. My God is a God of Grace. He loves me unconditionally, accepts me fully, and forgives me completely. I am not deserving of this grace, but through my faith, I receive it. I am a Christian. I believe Jesus is the son of God who died for my sins and was raised from the dead. I believe God clears a path before me, walks as a companion beside me, and dwells within me. He never leaves me. Some days I just forget to open the door to invite Him in. In my life, God spoke to me once. I was sitting at a table by myself reading the Bible, and these words rang in my ears. They were nowhere on the written page, and I did not say them, so I hurried to write them down:

**"Give not what you cannot fulfill, but give what you have and hold fast."**

I have thought about these words many, many times. I think they are a statement of humility, and I am holding fast to my God.

**Chapter Eleven Notes**

1. Oliver J. Morgan and Merle Jordan, *Addiction and Spirituality: A Multidisciplinary Approach* (St. Louis: Chalice Press, 1999).

2. American Journal of Psychiatry. 2008. *Spirituality, Evidence-Based Medicine, and Alcoholics Anonymous* [online]. Available from http://ajp.psychiatryonline.org/cgi/content/full/165/12/1514 (accessed 5 September 2011).

3. Project MATCH Research Group. 1998. Matching alcoholism treatment to client heterogeneity: Project MATCH three-year drinking outcomes. *Alcoholism: Clinical and Experimental Research* 22(6), 1300–1311.

4. Corrine Hyman and PJ Hardal. 2006. Pilot study. *Journal of Religion and Health.*

# CHAPTER TWELVE

# The Addict and the Chief Enabler

*No one thing a person says or*
*does can make an addict use.*

At the heart of understanding the disease of addiction as a family illness is an understanding of the relationship between the addict and chief enabler. What is meant by the term *chief enabler*? The chief enabler is the person who is most responsible for cushioning the fall, rescuing the addict or bailing him or her out of trouble, taking on the addict's responsibilities, and trying to control his or her addiction. This can happen in a number of ways. The chief enabler— whether that person is a spouse, parent, child, or friend of the addict—may rescue the addict financially, sometimes over and over. The enabler may rescue the addict emotionally by forgiving or trusting him or her again for the thousandth time, even when it makes absolutely no sense. The enabler may cover for the addict's absenteeism, tardiness, and poor performance at work. The enabler may pay for treatment after treatment for the addiction when, at some point, the addict needs to assume total responsibility for the consequences of the addiction.

When I give a lecture during family week, I always hesitate to use the word *sickness* when talking about the behavior of family members. So often, family members, unless they have already been exposed to recovery meetings or some form of healthy addiction-based therapy, see the addict as the only person in the family who has become sick. I often use a role-play to approach the issue of the enabler also having a sickness. I will pick a female at random out of the audience and have her come forward to stand beside me. I ask her to play the role of my daughter who is just beginning to be active in her addiction. I then ask the audience to pretend that there is a tiny ditch between us that is only six inches wide and six inches deep, and it represents the first problem that my daughter—let's call her Tina, age sixteen—has in her addiction. But to cross the ditch requires Dad's help.

Suppose this first problem is that Dad found beer cans hidden under Tina's bed. He questions her. Tina tells Dad her friend's boyfriend drinks and put them in his girlfriend's backpack. She must have put them under the bed. Tina swears it's the truth and that she doesn't drink. Dad believes her; she grasps Dad's hand and steps easily over the ditch. Because addiction is a progressive disease, as Tina's drinking continues, more problems happen, and there are more confrontations with Dad, who now knows Tina is drinking. Yet there is little in the way of negative consequences, because she promises to quit and invariably says, "Dad, if you love me, you'll trust me." Meanwhile, the ditch is getting deeper. Somewhere down the road, Tina calls from jail—not her first time there for a DUI. She begs her father to bail her out. By now, her mother won't talk to her. Tina has moved in and out of the house depending on when she needs money. When Dad answers the phone, he is angry, hurt, frightened, and confused. He shouts, "You did this to yourself; just stay there." His daughter cries, "You don't care about me." Then she pauses and says, "Oh, Daddy, I'm so scared. I'm in a room with a lot of other people who could hurt me. If you love me, please get me out of here." And he does.

Tina is still standing opposite me at the front of the room. To represent getting her out of jail, she reaches for my hand to cross the ditch, but instead, she falls into a canyon and dies.

**With the disease of addiction, no one
knows when the ditch becomes a canyon.**

I then turn to the audience and ask, "Who is sicker? Is it Tina on one side of the ditch, or her father on the other?" The reality is that both are sick. The father's intentions are good. He loves his daughter and wants her safe. But his sickness is his inability to allow her to fall in the ditch while it is still a ditch and deal with the negative consequences of her addiction.

Now, let me be very clear about something here. I am not talking about fault or blame where either person is concerned. Usually one of the first things I do when meeting with a group of family members of addicts is let them know that I am one of them. I then go on to tell them that I know many of them have been or still are living in their own private hell, thinking that no one can really understand what they have been through and what they are still feeling. I tell them that I know that they are glad their family member is in treatment, but there is a part of them that is saying, "What about me? I'm exhausted. I'm left to deal day-to-day with the destruction caused by the addiction. I don't know how to quit, and I don't know how to ask for help." As I say these words, there are usually some tears in the audience, just from their feeling understood.

## Qualities of the Chief Enabler

- Is self-critical

- Has a hard time saying no without feeling guilty

- Needs to be in control

- Appears independent

- Has a basic need to take care of someone

- Tries to be responsible for someone else's happiness

- Has a difficult time asking for help

- Is often a talker, but has difficulty risking feelings

- Has no idea how to be good to him- or herself

- Is a hard worker, performance oriented

## Qualities of the Active Addict

- Is into self, or is selfish

- Has a basic need to be taken care of by others

- Blames others

- Tends to play role of being bitter and/or victim

- Needs problems

- Tends to be untrusting

- Thinks he or she can manage the disease

- Is drawn to conflict and chaos

- Is increasingly isolated

- Is dependent

Let's discuss the characteristics of the enabler first. When I ask the audience to name a one-word feeling to describe what this person's life would be like, the following are the most frequent replies: exhausted, miserable, depressed, lonely, crazy. Invariably, one of the family members will ask, "Was I born this way, or did this disease of addiction make me this way?" My answer, first, is to say that many of the qualities on the list are actually very positive, such as being nurturing, persevering, and hardworking; having leadership and organizational skills; being compassionate; and having good verbal skills. Next, I reinforce the fact that these qualities and this way of living have allowed many people in the audience to achieve many things and have worked well in their lives. In a nutshell, most enablers always believed that if they just worked hard enough and loved enough, things would work out—until they ran headfirst into the disease of addiction. At that point, they began to carry those positive qualities to an extreme in trying to fix the addict, and in their doing so, the qualities became unhealthy and part of their sickness.

As for the list for the addict, it's important to remember that it is a list describing a person who is active in his or her disease, not what that person is necessarily like when clean and sober.

Often when I would give this lecture at a conference, I would title it "Moth to a Flame." The reason for this is that one person's sickness reinforces the other person's sickness. Here are some examples from the above lists:

1.  The enabler tends to be self-critical, and the addict tends to blame others. Therefore, when the addict blames his enabling wife for something, she automatically assumes it's her fault because of her self-critical nature.

2.  The addict has a basic need for someone to take care of him or her, and the enabler has a basic need to take care of someone. Therefore, the addict's dependency and the enabler's control are reinforced.

3.  The enabler tries to be responsible for someone's happiness, and the addict needs problems. What a recipe for disaster and endless manipulation on the part of the addict. The enabler doesn't know how to quit, and therefore will continue to fight a battle that is impossible to win.

4. The enabler tends to be hardworking and performance oriented, and the addict becomes increasingly isolated and into self. Thus, the addict has less interaction with the family and the enabler takes on more and more exhausting responsibilities at home.

The following chart shows the characteristics of the addict and enabler again, but this time both lists appear with qualities rearranged so that each number illustrates how a given characteristic in one individual reinforces the sickness in the other individual.

| Enabler | Addict |
|---|---|
| 1. Needs to take care of someone | 1. Needs to be taken care of |
| 2. Controlling, independent | 2. Dependent |
| 3. Self-critical | 3. Blames others |
| 4. Responsible for others' happiness | 4. Needs problems |
| 5. Hard time asking for help | 5. Selfish |
| 6. Talks a lot, hard worker | 6. Isolated |
| 7. Hard time saying no | 7. Self-centered |
| 8. Can't express feelings | 8. Nontrusting |

I hope you can see that as long as both people stay active in the family disease, the relationship becomes more and more enmeshed, and each person loses more and more of his or her own identity.

> **Most frightening of all is that this family
> disease of addiction is a disease of denial,
> and neither the addict nor the enabler has
> any real insight into the sickness of their
> thinking or behavior.**

After pointing all this out to family members, both addicts and enablers, I realize this can paint a somewhat depressing picture. It's then that I explain that often all it takes is one person getting into recovery to change the dynamics of the family disease.

Sometimes, particularly with couples, people wish things wouldn't change, but change is inevitable. If the enabler begins to attend recovery meetings that are meant to help friends and family members of the addict, and works on his or her own recovery, the enabler learns to accept that he or she is powerless over the addict and begins to work a one-day-at-a-time program. Typically, when addicts lose their enabler(s), they tend to reach bottom quicker in their addiction, which is sometimes necessary for them to finally reach out for help with recovery. The reverse is also true. When the addict gets into recovery and the enabler has always blamed the addict for all the problems in his or her life, the enabler is forced to look at the fact that he or she is just as miserable, but can no longer point the finger at the addict as the source of the problem. Ultimately, the enabler realizes the problem is within him- or herself, and that he or she needs help. Beneath the control, performance, and caretaking of the chief enabler is often poor self-esteem.

Early in my addiction work, on the unit where I was director we would have the patients elect a community leader. They usually chose a person based not on popularity, but more on whom they saw as being a positive force in the community and group process—someone serious about and committed to his or her recovery. At one time, there was a leader named Phillip. I walked on the unit one morning while Phillip was community leader, and I immediately knew something was very wrong. All the patients seemed upset, and the energy on the unit was low. I immediately called a group meeting. Before I went into the group, I learned from the head nurse that Phillip had jumped the fence and gone AWOL.

As I sat down in group, I asked each patient how he or she felt about Phillip leaving. The first patient said, "I'm angry. I trusted him. If he were here right now, I would bust him up." The next patient said, "I feel betrayed. We talked about so much and shared things. I guess I thought he wouldn't do this to me." The third patient said, "I feel hurt and abandoned. I'm so sad and feel rejected." The fourth patient said, "I'm frightened for him. Something must have happened for him to do this. It's just not like him." As I listened to all this, something dawned on me. I looked slowly around the group and then said, "With all the emotional pain in this room, you all as addicts are getting just an inkling of what it's like to be a family member in someone's long-term addiction—waiting by the telephone, looking out the window, and feeling hurt, betrayed, angry, afraid, and abandoned all at the same time." The room became quiet, and the patients spent the rest of the time talking not about Phillip but about their families.

In the late 1980s, I facilitated a weekly family aftercare group. Aftercare was a free group therapy session for people who had family members who had been patients of our treatment facility within the last ninety days. When I had a group of family members who were having a particularly hard time with understanding how their control issues and rigidity (fear of change) were hindering them from enjoying life and recovery, I found that playing the song "The Rose," sung by Bette Midler and written by Amanda McBroom, was a wonderful way to convey my message. I would give each of them a copy of the lyrics, and I found that often by the time we were halfway through, without my asking, they were singing along with tears in their eyes.

**Typically, the person the enabler resents the most is the addict.**

The addict sometimes has difficulty identifying resentments toward the enabler, but that is only true if the addict usually expresses hurt outwardly, not anger. The addict who expresses anger outwardly has no difficulty identifying resentments against the enabler. Typically, resentments by the addict are based on the fact that he or she knows, consciously or unconsciously, that to be able to use the way he or she wants to, there has to be someone there to take care of things, rescue him or her, and make excuses. In order to use the way he or she wants to, the addict is willing to give up certain things to the enabler. These include power and at times self-respect from allowing him- or herself to be yelled at, judged, or discounted. But that doesn't mean the addict doesn't resent it.

When working with patients, I explain that resentments are a natural part of this family disease and need to be dealt with in the presence of a third person, an addiction professional. Often the family members may have had little education regarding the disease when the addict returns home from inpatient treatment. Resentments surface frequently. I encourage my patients to apologize for their behavior in their addiction, but at some point to be able to say, "I understand your resentments, but I don't deserve this continued verbal abuse, so I'm going to leave the room now."

**The addict's recovery can't come from his or her enabler or family, and the enabler's recovery can't come from the addict.** They each need to work their own separate recovery program. Then their time spent together can be quality time, spent not talking about recovery but talking about the day, and each being out of self.

# CHAPTER THIRTEEN

# Childhood Roles

*"The three golden rules for children of alcoholic families are don't talk, don't trust, and don't feel."*

—*Claudia Black, PhD*

Twelve years ago I was struggling with a bout of worsening depression, and my therapist was convinced the solution was going back to deal with my childhood pain again. When I finally reluctantly agreed to do so, I told her I was uncertain how to get in touch with those feelings again. She asked me what I used as an outlet for feelings when I was younger. I mentioned sports, music, and poetry. When she asked about the poetry, I told her I had loved reading a book called *One Hundred and One Famous Poems*, and that I had also had written poetry. She suggested I try poetry as a way of connecting with my childhood again. I went home that evening, opened a small spiral notebook, and proceeded to write approximately twenty-two poems in a space of two days, taking time out only for work and to eat. It was strictly flow of consciousness, and it could not wait to get out.

I attended my first National Addiction Conference in 1983 in Clearwater, Florida. I was beginning to consider working in the field, although a lot of my own family and caretaking issues were far from resolved. One of the keynote speakers was Dr. Claudia Black. She had truly helped formulate and spearhead the Adult Children of Alcoholics movement. Her presentation that day included a discussion of childhood roles within the alcoholic family. This was all new information to me. She listed the different roles and discussed each one. There were probably twelve hundred or more people in attendance.

As she described these roles and I furiously took notes, I began to cry. I knew that what she was saying touched "old pain" deep within me, but my tears were not all of sadness. I realized later that day, after talking to some of the other participants, that maybe for the first time I had some idea of who I really was.

**I understood that a child takes on a role within a family in order to attempt to be safe, to survive, or to get needs met, and does this unconsciously at an early age.**

Knowing this, I was able to let go of some of the shame and guilt for my fears, past behaviors, and ways of dealing with things in particular situations, which were things I disliked about myself. I felt validated in a way that I never had before. Claudia had given me a gift that I have never forgotten, and she remains one of the people whom I see as a living legend in the field of addiction, having affected countless lives of survivors of addiction and trauma.

I identified myself as a hero child—constantly driven to perform with a high fear of failure. While I was excelling at sports, receiving accordion awards, being president of my senior class, or receiving some other honor, I was constantly going fast. I now think of myself back then as being inadequate and always fearful of something. But someone from my past whom I had not talked to in over forty years reminded me of what a big ego I had. I was both surprised and hurt by this. After I did some painful reflection, realizing that what that person had said was true emphasized for me how thick that shell of defense was in high school and how vague a memory it had become in my present life. As is so often the case with the hero child, I was the ultimate imposter, receiving award after award and never feeling deserving of any of them.

I also identified myself as being in the role of mascot/placater. I was the "peace at any cost" child in my family. I would do anything to avoid my father's verbal and sometimes physical rages. As my sister grew older, the yelling and screaming escalated to include her and my mother. At times my temper would flare, but seldom at home. As the placater, I demonstrated caretaking tendencies early on that would later dominate my early adult life and marriage. One of the most painful realizations that I made, after years of working with adult children from addicted homes in treatment who were mascot/placaters like me, was that too often we make decisions, even important ones, based on fear rather than what is best for us.

Later, after working with patients over the years, I went back and added the lost child role to my list, because I came to understand that any hero child who plays the role of imposter is ultimately lonely and carries a huge secret regarding his or her true feelings about self—fear of abandonment, guilt, and poor self-esteem. Over time these negative views, often combined with chronic anxiety and depression, become even more distorted.

Last, I must add that the anger my father demonstrated became a part of my behavior after the birth of our first child. As is so often the case with adult children from dysfunctional homes, I swore I would never do that to my children; but it happened. Following my severe depression, my anger seemed to fade and has continued to do so over the years, but it is the part of me that for years I hated the most.

Before we review the five basic childhood roles in depth, let me say that my definition and use of the different roles are really a mixture of Claudia Black's and my own experience.

There is another list that is important to mention, and that is Claudia Black's Three Golden Rules for Adult Children of Alcoholics:[1]

1. **Don't Talk.** (If I don't talk, I don't get yelled at, ignored, hit, etc.) The child is also reminded to keep the family's secrets regarding addiction or other problems. This reinforces the denial within the family. This "don't talk" rule keeps a child believing that his or her family is okay, but

at the same time keeps him or her at a high level of constant stress and hypervigilance. Pretending the elephant in the living room is not there, even when it is getting bigger and creating more problems, gets harder and harder. The rule of silence dominates the two remaining rules in terms of its long-term influence on the child.

2.  **Don't Trust.** (If I don't trust, then I won't be disappointed again when my father doesn't show up for my sixth baseball game in a row, or when my mother promises to help with my homework but is passed out on the couch from taking too many pills.) With this lack of trust comes a huge fear of abandonment, which I will discuss in more detail later. With the lack of trust, the child unconsciously begins to assemble his or her own often rigid rules for living in an attempt to be safe and in control.

3.  **Don't Feel.** (If all I'm going to feel is hurt, anger, and fear, I'll just "numb out" and not feel anything.) Sometimes the term used for this is psychic numbing. It is not uncommon for adults in treatment for addiction to have not only fear of risking feelings, but also the inability to identify feelings and an unclear view of self.

All of the above rules certainly leave a child from this family unprepared for a healthy intimate adult relationship.

In working with adults who grew up in addicted homes and with addicts who have children, I always tell them that there are two things children need:

1. **They need *love*.**

2. **They need *answers*.**

They are more likely to get love from at least one parent than they are to get answers. Children see all these crazy things happening in their homes, and no one comes back and explains what it means. Dad, in a drunken state, punches his fist through a wall; Mom takes the kids to live at her mother's for a week, then goes back home; a bicycle is run over in the driveway and is thrown away, and no explanation is given. Usually the child sees Mom and Dad angry and thinks somehow it's his or her fault. With no answers to life's daily questions, children slowly learn to rely on themselves and trust no one. Their shame, low self-esteem, isolation, fear of abandonment, and tolerance for inappropriate behavior are all affected by this.

Returning now to the subject of childhood roles, I will present them in the way that I would as a lecture to a group of seventy impaired professionals at Talbott Recovery Campus, where I have lectured in the past. While childhood roles were originally talked about in relation to adult children from alcoholic homes, in my experience they are applicable to every family. The intensity of the roles may vary, but the roles are always present.

I ask the audience to think of childhood roles as a framework, like many others—as a tool to elicit important therapeutic, traumatic, and family insight, as well as to gain an understanding of the rules of survival or coping for a given patient.

I believe every child has two basic needs:

1. **The need to be safe** (represented by an asterisk [*] in the following list);

2. **The need to get other basic needs met** (physical affection [hugs], approval, attention, love, not to be discounted; represented by a box [ □ ] in the following list).

## The Five Childhood Roles

1. **The Hero * □**
   This is the child who is performance oriented, who goes fast as a means of avoiding feelings, and in this way feels safe. The hero child wears the family badge of honor, as if to say, "Look how good I'm doing; there can't be anything wrong with my family." Hero children get their needs met through approval for their accomplishments, present a good image for the family, and usually don't cause trouble. While appearing often as the "looking-good kid" or as "nothing going on here," inwardly the hero child often feels unworthy or inadequate and fearful. Hero children play the role of the imposter with the combination of an increased ego and decreased self-esteem. They are prone

to anxiety and depression. Their greatest fear is of doing something wrong. They tend to feel overly responsible for the family, and have a need to be right, but at the same time they don't always trust their own perceptions. Despite their notoriety, they feel very isolated.

2.  **The Lost Child \***
    This is the child who unconsciously learns that the only way to survive is to be invisible and "blend into the woodwork." Lost children are quiet, are nonassertive, may or may not perform well in school, and have little expectations of family. Everything is centered on the need to be safe, but they are getting no other needs met. Often feeling ignored by parents or siblings, they may choose to create a world of their own. Lost children are less likely to seek help even as adults, and because of the lack of dialogue with others, struggle with identifying feelings, much less risking them. They may also be more prone to sexual identity problems.

3.  **The Mascot/Placater \* □**
    This is the "peace-at-any–cost" child who will do anything to avoid anger or conflict. Mascot/placater children are getting the need to be safe met. They are often Mommy's or Daddy's little helper. They will also take on the role of comedian to defuse a potentially volatile situation. If they predominantly play the role of

comedian, they may not be taken seriously by family or peers. They may demonstrate a lot of caretaking features early on, and in an addicted household, they may pattern their behavior after the enabling parent. They may end up marrying an addict in their adult life. Mascot/ placater children's other needs are being met because they often receive appreciation for the help they give. They do not cause trouble, and may be mediators in the family. Mascot/placater children operate under an incredible level of fear, and often make decisions based on fear rather than what is best for them.

4. **The Scapegoat** ☐

   This is the child in the family who is basically blamed for everything, who is the black sheep or the troublemaker. If Joey is the scapegoat in his family and a glass breaks in the kitchen, by the time it hits the floor everybody yells "Joey did it," even though Joey is not at home. It's debated whether children subconsciously choose their role(s) or the dynamics of the family place a child in a particular role. I believe it varies and is a combination of both. Scapegoat children never really feel safe since they are getting "hammered" every day verbally or physically, but they are getting some needs met in terms of attention, although the attention is generally negative. The scapegoat is usually the child who is most honest about what is really going on in the family. The scapegoat is often the means in the family to divert attention from the real problem (for instance, Dad's addiction). There can be a lot of self-destructive behavior and self-hatred in these children, but they are often the first to seek treatment.

5.  **The Hyperactive Child □ \***
    When talking about these children, I feel the need to separate them into two categories: those with disabilities and those without. Children with disabilities like AD/HD, disorders of written expression, and so on, have hyperactivity in large part as a result of their disability. However, there is a second group of children without disabilities but with hyperactivity who unconsciously choose this role as an attempt to be safe and get needs met. By going fast, hyperactive children do not have to slow down and feel, which unconsciously offers a way to feel safe. Also, by always being somewhat mischievous without being malicious, they demand attention, which they get.

In talking about the above five roles, you will notice that there are two roles where children only get one of the two basic needs met. These are the lost child and the scapegoat. The lost child has some feeling of safety, but gets no other needs met. The scapegoat feels little or no safety, but gets some attention or other needs met, albeit mostly in negative ways. These are also the two roles where children tend to leave the family at the earliest age and turn to peers, looking to fill those needs not met by the family. Unfortunately, what they find outside the family are other lost children and scapegoats, and a much-increased incidence of addiction. Over the years I have asked adolescent inpatients what role or roles they identify for themselves, and 80 percent identify lost child and/or scapegoat as one of the roles they play. It is not surprising, given the above information.

When looking at childhood roles as an adult, it is important to note that you may have had one or more than one role, or your roles may have changed. There are some common patterns. I often see the pattern of hero and mascot/placater. This is common among impaired physicians and other professionals. When I hear patients identify themselves first as lost, then as hero, I am quick to ask them at what age they became the hero, and in what niche they found themselves. I have a friend who was a lost child and grew up in his church, but at age sixteen he found he had a real talent as a speaker, and he quickly stepped into the role of hero.

When I have patients identify themselves as hero or mascot, then scapegoat or lost child, I ask them questions such as "What age were you when things changed, and what happened at that time?" "Is that when your addiction began?" "Did your parents divorce?" "Was there a move where you were forced to leave all your friends?"

It is not unusual for patients to identify themselves with all five roles. I have seen this in children with chaotic families, where they try each role in an attempt to be noticed or accepted, and afterward, in adult life, they continue to be like the chameleon lizard, changing colors to be the person a particular situation or person requires without a truly clear sense of self. I have also seen it in only children who try to be all things to their parents.

I tell my patients and audiences that the role(s) that are still present are often a part of the fabric of who they are. They will not likely change that completely. But most things in recovery are about progress, not perfection. It is a willingness to work on making positive changes in these roles that is essential. That being said, the following is a list of areas to work on to make positive changes specific to each role.

## Focuses for Changes in Childhood Roles

1. **The Hero**

   Hero children's greatest fear is often doing something wrong, and they are extremely self-critical. They must work on allowing themselves their own humanity. In other words, they must work on humility.

   One of the most important tasks I assign adult hero children in treatment is to write down how they truly see themselves, not how they portray themselves to the outside world. They are asked to do this in one sitting, and are assured that no one else will see it but me, unless they choose otherwise. I ask that they not reread or rewrite it, but merely sign their name, fold it up, and bring it to me the next morning for me to read back to them. This is usually a painful and fear-inducing assignment. Yet in sharing their secrets and distorted view of themselves with me, they feel no rejection, abandonment, or belief in any

of the description they give. Instead, I explain, as
I did prior to the assignment, that the image they
have of themselves is built on the shame and guilt
they assumed as children, feeling responsible for
the dysfunction in their families. I also explain
that they have attributed needs that were not met
in childhood to their being not good enough or
somehow unworthy, rather than recognizing the
truth—that it was not about them, but rather the
sickness within their parents and their parents'
inability to meet some of their needs. I remind
them that all children are innocent. The relief,
and often the tears, that follow are a major step
toward recovery.

Another major area of work for the hero child
is to become a good listener, and that means
slowing down as well. Most hero children use
intellectualization, talking a lot, and going fast
as ways to "stuff" feelings. One of the best ways
to slow down and work on talking less is to be
silent in group process, except to express a one-
word feeling of either hurt, fear, or anger. As
mentioned previously, the way to become a better
listener is to practice being silent until a person is
completely finished talking and then respond by
saying only "I hear you."

A final area of work for the hero child in recovery
involves taking a parent or other family member
off a pedestal. You can see this same dynamic in

several of the other childhood roles, and it is an attempt to create an idealized family rather than recognize the reality of life at home. Typically, a child will put a parent on a pedestal and associate the words *right, perfect,* and *strong* with him or her. Then that parent becomes an unconscious daily focus for the child, who attempts to be as "perfect" as the parent is. This is a recipe for failure and creates poor self-esteem, often despite outstanding performance in school, sports, or other areas.

Identifying this dynamic is important in recovery, since in this world of pedestals there is no room for God. When these children get in trouble, even God does not surpass perfection, so it is not God's face they see, but that of the person on the pedestal. The crux of the matter is that the person on the pedestal must come down before the adult child, who is beneath them trying to climb up, can come down. The best means I know of to help patients with this issue is to encourage them to see that person on the pedestal as God might see him or her—not perfect, right, and strong, but a struggling child of God with imperfections and a basic need for help from a higher power. By taking the parent off the lofty, unrealistic perch they have stood upon since the person's childhood, the person in treatment gains a tremendous sense of relief and may have the primary stumbling block to both surrender and spirituality for this hero child removed.

## 2. The Lost Child

When helping lost children in recovery in the inpatient setting, it is crucial to first understand that they may have difficulty identifying feelings as well as risking them. Particular attention must be paid to these patients to ensure that, although they are typically compliant and don't cause problems in treatment, they are not allowed to slip through treatment without working on their painful issues. Within their family of origin, lost children often feel discounted and of little value, and tend to operate from a place of low self-esteem. Lost children often will not voluntarily seek outpatient therapy, but instead will present in crisis in an inpatient setting with addiction or depression or both.

In addition to having the highest rates of addiction, lost children and scapegoats are the two most common roles seen in inpatient adolescent psychiatric hospitals. Helping lost children first and foremost requires making them feel safe and cared about in their environment, whether inpatient or outpatient. They must come to understand that they unconsciously took on a role, or were forced into a role by the dynamics of the family, and their only solace was some sense of safety they got by creating a fantasy world that was theirs alone. The lost child is not the person that his or her dysfunctional family script has depicted.

Lost children are often good students, and as adults may end up in professions such as acting or writing because of their creativity. In treatment, I make lost children a promise to care about them, and I explain the importance of journaling and how writing things down helps make them real. As with all patients, but especially with lost children, I am always attuned to the possibility of previously undisclosed physical or sexual abuse because these children are frequently nonassertive, have difficulty with boundaries, and are often left unattended. They are unlikely to talk about the trauma in their home, where their needs seem to have been forgotten.

I help lost children with identifying feelings as I explain core feelings and the need to make the hard choices in treatment. Because lost children often do not have a clear sense of self and have a tendency to be avoidant, I ask that they trust me when I tell them that if they use a twelve-step facilitated form of recovery as their guide to finding themselves, they are going to like the person they find, as I already have. Since low self-esteem is such a major issue in lost children, if they have any sense of a higher power or God, I remind them that in my God's eyes they are bright, shining, lovable, and special. Then, many times, they walk into group, and for the first time they hear people talk openly about their problems and addiction, and they feel accepted. Lost children need continued individual therapy and support groups to have a safe place where people affirm them and identify with their emotional pain as they work on their recovery.

3.  **The Mascot/Placater**

    Mascot children are often the comedians in the family, and may drift into adulthood with little change. They may have a tendency to stay stuck in this childhood role and be slow to take on the responsibilities of adult life. Like all children from dysfunctional families, they fear intimacy and have had little modeling on how to express their true feelings or be vulnerable. They tend to be followers, not leaders. For mascots to become emotionally responsible for themselves and to lose their fear of abandonment, they must work a daily recovery program, with commitment to doing it someone else's way. They must realize that people can be there for them, not just when they are laughing, but when they are not okay.

    On the other hand, children who act primarily in the placater role tend to operate from an incredible place of fear, doing anything to avoid conflict or anger. They often pattern their helping and caretaking behavior after the spouse of the addict in their family of origin, and it is not unusual for them to marry an addict. Placater children are prone to anxiety and depression. With an overdeveloped sense of responsibility and an oversized conscience, they tend to be extremely hard workers, and are often found in the helping professions. Helper children need to work on control issues, which are based on a fear of being vulnerable, and on learning to be responsible to people, not for them, as well as giving up the need to be right. They often need individual therapy, and may also need medical treatment for depression when it is indicated. Like hero children, they have an incredibly hard time asking for help, and, like most children in dysfunctional families, must learn how to be good to themselves and have fun. They are prone to enmeshed relationships and need to work diligently on having their own space and claiming their own identity.

In my experience, the only true cure for placater children's overwhelming anger and fear of people is spiritual.

The mascot/placater combination children are capable of a full range of emotions, and humor can serve as a positive attribute in their lives. Anytime there is a lot of repressed anger beneath the fear, as is often the case with this family role, Gestalt or experiential therapy, with family sculpting or other techniques, can be extremely helpful when done by an experienced professional. This can include doing family sculptures or other forms of role playing, use of a batanka bat to physically express repressed anger in a safe fashion with the encouragement of the patient community, guided imagery, and so on.

4. **The Scapegoat**
The scapegoat's road to recovery is a difficult one, just as with the rest of the childhood roles; however, this role does have one unique feature as it relates to addiction. Scapegoat children in the dysfunctional family tend to leave the family sooner, usually to get their needs met from peers because their needs are not being met at home. They leave the home situation physically, feeling like the victim of the family and angry and bitter about their role growing up. Unfortunately, this is the same role addicts play unconsciously in their active addiction. Therefore, treating adult scapegoat children usually means making them aware of when they slip back into the role of victim or feeling bitterness in their addictive thinking. They are prone to blaming others for what's wrong and to carrying resentments, which are the number-one cause of relapse.

I help scapegoat children through written assignments dealing with their resentments, but more importantly, with the hurt beneath their anger. The adult scapegoat often still suffers from a lot of self-loathing and may be self-destructive in his or her life choices, either consciously or unconsciously. A part of scapegoat children has never understood why they were the "bad seed," and their heart has always felt, despite their resentments, that there must be something wrong with them, so they are filled with shame.

Structure and authority are usually difficult for scapegoats, and it is not unusual for them to have had legal problems by the time they get to treatment. In treatment we focus on daily tools of recovery, surrender, and slowing down. Scapegoat children are often easy targets for bullying, as are lost children. Although trust is difficult for them, because of their ability to take risks, in recovery they are capable of finding a way of thinking that is positive and spiritual through a twelve-step facilitated program.

5. **The Hyperactive Child**
In order to receive the maximum help in recovery, adults who were hyperactive children must first address any underlying untreated disabilities such as AD/HD, dyslexia, disorders of written expression, and so forth. Next, by far the most important step is to slow down and begin to follow a routine or structure, one day at a time—just what a twelve-step facilitated program recommends.

Going fast has been a way for hyperactive children to both get attention and not have to feel emotional pain within them. The hyperactivity will have subsided in some of these children by adulthood, but the fear of abandonment, low self-esteem, shame, trust issues, and fear of intimacy are still left in place. Hyperactive children often have a good work ethic, but may struggle with taking this to an extreme of not being good to themselves. Also, boundary issues often need to be a focus in treatment. In the absence of a severe disability that is untreated, hyperactive children may do well as adults in the business world, unless addiction surfaces.

For counselors, social workers, nurses, physicians, and other professionals, a working knowledge of childhood roles can be extremely helpful in understanding the underlying motivations behind behaviors. For each of us as human beings, understanding our childhood roles can be a source of validation—without fault or blame placed anywhere—for who we are, of recognizing the origin of some of our patterns of thinking and behavior, and of a way to go about working on recovery.

**Chapter Thirteen Notes**

1. Claudia Black, *It Will Never Happen to Me* (New York: Ballantine Books, 1986).

# CHAPTER FOURTEEN

# Finding a Purpose in the Pain

*"Better than a thousand hollow words is one word that brings peace."*

——

—*The Buddha*

This chapter is based on a lecture I give of the same name that is invariably the most emotionally exhausting for me to present to patients. This probably derives from the fact that it stimulates so much of my personal pain. The origin of this lecture goes back more than twenty years. In my practice, I became increasingly aware of addicts who presented to treatment in a great deal of distress, and during the course of their stay never seemed to connect to the program of recovery, would relapse, or sometimes ended up dying from their addiction. It was as if they went through fear, hurt, and anger, but found only the solution of numbing out again with alcohol or other drugs. In effect, they could never find a purpose in their emotional pain. This caused me to look earnestly at the benefits to myself and many of my patients who chose to risk and even embrace the pain rather than avoid it, and follow a twelve-step program. Below are ten "purposes in the pain" that I have found to be invaluable.

1. **Pain allows others to be there for you.** Most of us are great at looking good on the outside, even when we are "dying emotionally" on the inside. Our fear of appearing weak or vulnerable is usually the underlying cause for this. However, when our emotional pain is so great, it cannot be hidden, and our tears fall like water over the top of a dam whether we like it or not. What's ironic about this is that our greatest fear is that if we lose control and expose our fear, tears, or anger, people will reject us, not want to be with us, and never see us the same way. In fact, just the opposite is true. Another way of saying it is this: never compare your "insides" to someone else's "outsides." This kind of comparing often arises when a patient is struggling mightily in treatment, with crying spells and fear, and comes to me asking why so many other patients are so much further along in their recovery. I explain that the patient who looks good outwardly may actually be less in touch with his or her pain and may have accomplished less in treatment thus far.

**It is when we are vulnerable that
people will reach out to us the most.**

I use the example of walking into a room with only two people in it. One person appears disinterested, bored, as if waiting for something. The other is sitting with her hands over her face, sobbing uncontrollably. Who are you going to be drawn to? In lecture group, 100 percent of the audience answers the girl who is sobbing and in need. Thus, pain allows others to be there for us.

A much more personal example involves the night I entered acute psychiatric treatment in December 1984. My wife and our friends, Larry and Becky, had driven me there in the middle of the night. I was feeling frightened, hopeless, and like a total failure. While my wife was getting me admitted, I was alone in a room and Larry walked in. I was so lonely, and because of my pain I did something I had never done in my life. I asked Larry if he would be my friend. I was crying as he said he would and that he already was, and he asked that I be his friend also. We hugged. That was twenty-six years ago, and since that day we have introduced each other to others as "my best friend Jim" and "my best friend Larry." We have remained best friends in the truest sense of the word since that moment of pain and vulnerability so many years ago.

2.  **Pain allows for major life change.** As my mentor Dr. Bill Simpson used to say, "Jim, we all go down screaming," meaning that most of us cling to what is familiar even if it is destructive or painful, because our fear of

change or of being alone is so great. With
addicts, we talk about hitting a "bottom." Often
this means reaching a point where someone is
living for their addictive behavior, and there
seems to be no way out. When someone finally
reaches a point where "anything has got to be
better than this," major change can occur. Thus,
emotional pain offers the opportunity for major,
positive change, a great example being getting
into recovery. Major life change is often needed
in our lives because, unless a painful life crisis
occurs, we will choose to continue on a familiar
course even though it may mean staying in
an abusive relationship cycle or a dead-end
job with a verbally abusive boss. While the
transition may be frightening and difficult, with
the help of God and a recovery program based
on taking things one day at a time, the results
will be worth it.

The fear of the unknown is a huge issue for anyone contemplating a major change in his or her life. For the addict, learning to live life on life's terms without the option of mood-altering substances as a quick fix is a scary proposition. Stepping out of the role of the angry victim and becoming an accountable and responsible member of the family while discovering what is left of his or her old identity can only be accomplished one day at a time, with the help of a higher power.

For many, this major life change may be based on a decision to put God and spirituality first in their lives. Giving less priority to worldly things and more to a spiritual path is a huge decision, and one usually made in the midst or aftermath of a crisis.

**Most human beings seldom, if ever, make major life changes except out of pain.**

3. **Pain allows us to find a better understanding of our identity.** So much of who I am as a person has been shaped by the struggles in my life. When we are in a great deal of emotional pain, we tend to wrestle with important questions about our self—that is, who we are, not just what we do. In these situations, we often enlist the help of professionals who can give us tools to explore our feelings and core beliefs. Much of this work often means going back and dealing with issues of family origin. It could, for instance, involve looking at a conflicted relationship with a parent where there are feelings of guilt, anger, and fear. Sharing these feelings with a trained professional may give new insight into a family sickness, relieve guilt, and give you a clear awareness that it's okay to be angry and that as a child you were innocent and none of it was your fault.

Many times painful acceptance is a part of finding your own identity. It could mean coming to grips with the fact that your father was an alcoholic or that the mother whom you have repeatedly gone to all these years hoping to hear the words "I love you" will probably never say them. But when you accept these things, it can open doors, in the first case, to explaining your lack of trust and code of silence, and in the second, to knowing that it was never about you being unlovable, but about your mother's sickness.

This could be the beginning of a major step toward recovery and improved self-esteem. Being in pain forces us to slow down, and it is in this setting that we can begin to gain a clearer picture of ourselves, our beliefs, and our relationships.

4. **Pain allows the opportunity to lessen, put an end to, or find closure for "old pain."** It has been my experience that regardless of what the present crisis or emotional pain that brings an addict to treatment is, as he or she proceeds through individual and group therapy, and once he or she is open to feelings, invariably old pain surfaces as well. In lectures, when I ask for a show of hands of how many patients have found this to be true, at least 90 percent raise their hands. In my case, when I was dealing with my major depression in 1985—rooted, I thought, in my caretaking and workaholism—a lot of my childhood verbal and physical abuse surfaced, as well as feelings of distance and lack of affection from my mother.

A special area that I am attuned to is the frequency of unidentified sexual abuse in my patients, even with previous psychiatric hospitalizations. When I identify this, my main focus is not an attempt to treat the abuse. Instead I educate adults who were victims of childhood sexual abuse on the many ways it has affected them in their adult life as it relates to depression, poor self-esteem, sexuality, trust, and other issues. Foremost, I assure them that they were victims and were innocent, that the guilt they have carried is unfounded. I explain that they will need long-term individual psychotherapy by someone who has true expertise in that field. However, I also explain that if those issues are not at the surface they do not have to be dealt with immediately, and I instruct them to keep their focus on treating the addiction.

5. **Pain allows us to get spiritually connected or reconnected.** Addicts often present to treatment in a state of being "spiritually bankrupt." In other words, as alcohol or other drugs become their overriding obsession and the center of their world, God ends up taking a backseat and the addict becomes more and more into self. Then, when at his or her bottom and in the midst of the pain, the addict is shown a program of surrender to a power greater than him- or herself. In a broader view, when I think of someone lost, in crisis, and in fear, I can imagine that person walking through a jungle, and by accident falling into a tiger trap that is twenty feet square and twenty feet deep, with no way out and in the middle of nowhere. After

considering all the options and unsuccessfully attempting to climb out, what is the person in the bottom of the trap most likely to do? The answer is cry for help. We may not call him God, but we are definitely calling to something outside ourselves. Pain can be the beginning of a spiritual connection or reconnection.

I grew up in a very strict church. By high school I had decided I could never be good enough to go to their heaven, and I saw many of the members as judgmental hypocrites. In the process, I stepped away from God. It was not until I had gone through my personal trials and pain and recovery that I was able to find God, a God of Grace that I could live with.

6. **Pain allows us to get our priorities in line.**
   When people are in severe emotional distress, all the little worries and material things that seemed to be important suddenly lose their value. People often say that you don't know how important your health is until you lose it. As someone who has lost his mental health in the past, I know the validity of that statement. At my worst, I prayed just to get through another day, not to have another panic attack, and to be able to be with my wife and children again. When an addict is "coming up for air" from the depths of his or her addiction, priorities are clear—priorities like physical and mental health, family, true friends, and God.

7. **Pain allows us to be grateful for simple blessings.** The best way to explain this is to tell a story regarding my own psychiatric hospitalization. For much of the first week or more, I was either having a panic attack, in the bed crying, or feeling nonfunctional. Finally, after I began taking some medication about two weeks into my stay, they told me to go to occupational therapy. This meant going outside for the first time. I had begun to feel somewhat better. When I walked outside, there was a breeze blowing. The feel of that breeze blowing on my face was one of the greatest feelings in my life. I can still feel it as I write this. You see, I realized in that moment that it was the first time I had been able to enjoy anything in a very long time. I see the gratitude on patients' faces all the time as they begin to experience relief from severe depression or the relief that comes after taking the healthy risk of sharing a painful written assignment with me.

To be truly grateful, you must take a one-day-at-a-time attitude and be open to finding God's blessings in each encounter of the day, in each opportunity that presents itself, or in just enjoying the view.

8. **Pain allows for relief from repressed hurt and anger.** In the chapter on feelings I explained how most of us have an easier time expressing either hurt or anger outwardly. For those of us who

have an easier time expressing anger outwardly, if our emotional pain gets great enough, our repressed hurt will come spilling out whether we want it to or not, and with those tears will come some relief. The opposite is true for those of us who express hurt more easily. When the pain is overwhelming, the anger will surface, at times explosively, but with this outward expression of anger can also come relief.

Most importantly, when we are in pain we need to realize that if anger is easiest for us to express, we must consciously work on getting out our repressed hurt and fear in treatment. The opposite is true if we express hurt outwardly with greater ease.

9. **Pain can allow us to understand humility.** I've described humility in this book as allowing ourselves and others humanity or "humanness." This means no one is better than anyone else. Judgment has no place with humility. Being in severe emotional pain and sharing that with others typically brings that group conscience to a place of humility, with each person focused not on judging the other, but on being a part of the emotional whole. Emotional pain is emotional pain; the outward trappings of an individual do not change that.

10. **Pain can be a source of passion.** It certainly has been in my work. Study many of the great

writers, artists, and philosophers, and you will
see how their own personal pain served as a
source of passion in their work. I believe that
is also true of many of the professionals who
work in the field of addiction. It has been my
experience that it is the passion of the treating
professional that may be a major factor in first
gaining the trust of a patient. I often end my
lectures by picking a patient at random from the
audience and asking what it would be like if I
gave that patient a gift that would allow him or
her to do all the following things: let others be
there for you, understand yourself better, make
a positive major change in your life, lessen or
put an end to old pain, develop your spirituality,
set your priorities in line, be grateful for simple
things, get relief from repressed hurt or anger,
understand humility, and be more passionate
about life in general. I then say, "Do you want
this gift?" The answer is always yes. When I ask
the entire group, the answer is unanimously yes
as well. Then I say,

**"Great! You already have this gift. It is your
pain. Now all you have to do is embrace it
rather than avoid it, and share it with others
when it is at the surface, and you will reap
the benefits."**

# CHAPTER FIFTEEN

# Patience, Relief, and Peace

*"He that can have patience can have what he will."*

—*Benjamin Franklin*

**W**hen considering the conclusion to this book, I thought I would end it with the previous chapter, reflecting the book's title. However, I realized that I had yet to communicate three ultimate keys to the work I do and to finding a purpose in the pain:

1. **Patience**
2. **Relief**
3. **Peace**

First, let me address patience. From the standpoint of an addict on the heels of his or her active addiction, nothing is harder than being patient. Even as I talk passionately with addicts about how recovery works, I cannot promise them that their emotional pain will lessen today. Instead, I ask them to trust a process based on a belief system that is the exact opposite of their addictive behavior. When I ask them to be patient, I understand that initially they are dealing with the fear that occurs when they go from a place of "going fast" in their addiction to suddenly stopping and feeling out of control. Patience is also important because it goes hand in hand with slowing down and simplifying life, which are critical to the recovery process. Patience is almost always the right answer when it comes to decision making. Rarely has a poor decision been made by being patient, but many have occurred as a result of a reactive, hurried answer.

> **From a spiritual standpoint, patience, or
> "waiting" as it is often termed in the biblical
> sense, is intimately related to trust.**

Without trust, there can be no true faith, but with trust must come the ability to wait for things to happen in God's time, not in ours. Thankfully, however, *waiting is done just for today, where the solution to recovery and God's light both dwell.*

That brings us to the second key to finding a purpose in the pain. As I looked over the list of purposes in the pain, it dawned on me that the ultimate purpose must be the goal of twelve-step recovery—serenity, or peace of mind. Yet, when I thought about my day-to-day work with patients, I realized it is not peace I am trying to give them most often, but some measure of *relief*. I want to list some examples of this relief as a reference for you:

1.  Relief in accepting that addiction is an illness and not a moral weakness.

2.  Relief in knowing it's okay to hate things a loved one does and still love that person.

3.  Relief in finding out they had an untreated major depressive disorder that went undiagnosed for a long time, and that they will respond to medication and never have to go back to "that place" again.

4.  Relief when a physician like myself can tell them before they tell me exactly what it feels like in their depression to be "walking around in a shell," feeling disconnected and convinced that they can't explain to anyone just how terrible they feel.

5.  Relief from long-term unresolved grief when I ask them to write a letter, not to say good-bye, but to reestablish communication and tell the person they've lost how much they miss him or her and begin to share all the good memories.

6. Relief from getting family secrets off their chest that they have been carrying around for years and realizing they are not betraying the family, but being good to themselves.

7. Relief in "jumping off the cliff," or surrendering to being powerless and letting go of trying to manage their addiction.

8. Relief in writing a letter to an abusive parent and saying everything in it they ever wanted or needed to say or ask without fear of retaliation, and sharing it with someone, but knowing it will never be mailed and will remain confidential.

9. Relief that comes after sharing the imposter, not the hero, with a group and finding out just how special, courageous, and giving they truly are and what a distorted view of self they have carried as a burden all these years.

10. Relief from someone explaining the impact their childhood sexual abuse has had on their adult life (for example, blind rages, sexual promiscuity or not wanting sex at all, cycles of severe depression, low self-esteem, nightmares, flashbacks, gaps in childhood memories, dissociative episodes, or "cutting") and that none of it is their fault.

11. Relief from unexpressed hurt, fear, and anger by learning about core feelings and substituting hurt for anger, and vice versa.

12. Relief from the painful acceptance that some people in their family are just not going to be there for them, as they have wanted them to be for so long, and then relief from ultimately going beyond that acceptance to a place of forgiveness.

The third and final key to finding a purpose in the pain is *peace*. This peace is of a spiritual nature, and in most cases it is a result of working a twelve-step facilitated program leading to the insights and moments of relief like those mentioned above. Peace is also part of the process of recovery, but it requires action. In Chapter Ten, I talk about morning quiet time spent alone with my higher power, whom I call God. Making this time a priority is essential to life and recovery. For the addict who is new to the recovery process, prayer may seem awkward or superficial, but like many things in early recovery, if you take the action, the feelings will follow. If prayer is too uncomfortable for you for right now, then just be still and quiet for five minutes. If you have twelve-step literature, you can read it to help you with this. The important thing is to make time for God in silence; that creates opportunities for you to experience peace.

It is in my suffering that I have come closest to my God and have found a path to peace. Life is a struggle for each one of us, and every child needs a place to seek comfort and safety. Whenever I have been willing to increase my quiet time spent with God, I have found there is a general sense of increased peace, with a different view and less fear of the world we live in. Whenever patients of mine have increased the quiet time they spend with God, they have reported the same experience. It is significant that in the Bible, the book of Ephesians, Chapter Six talks about putting on the full armor of God to fight the daily struggles we face in a fallen world.

In my study of the Bible and in my own personal experience, I have noted how many times God has used the terms "hold fast" and "stand firm" when He talks about dealing with trials and difficult circumstances. When I think of standing firm, I must have my feet planted solidly in something I can trust to withstand the adversity I face. Chapter Six of Ephesians also describes the various parts of the armor, such as the belt of truth and the shield of faith, and the gospel of peace that the warrior's feet are firmly planted in. If a warrior cannot remain on his feet, it is difficult for him to win. If an individual cannot find some measure of spiritual peace, it is difficult to stay in today and experience the true feeling of recovery.

In a recovery meeting when someone is sharing a painful experience, the room is silent and the silence is "heavy." Although there is suffering for some in that room, for others there is a peace that is a result of remembering pain that brought them to a place of safety and love that will never disappear. My life to date has been a journey, often a fearful one, especially in my younger years. Then I found twelve-step recovery through my own pain as a family member of an addict, and by working in the field of addiction medicine. Over time, I learned the value of patience as a key to recovery and in my own life. I have certainly experienced moments of insight and enlightenment, which, along with my willingness to be vulnerable, have given moments of relief too numerous to count. But it has only been in the last two years that I have actively worked toward, and truly made time for, God.

> **I have found the true essence of my life and the purpose in my pain, and that is the peace and path I find in the time I spend alone with God each morning, reading, praying, meditating, and talking.**

In conclusion, it is my hope that this book can provide a helpful resource for professionals and nonprofessionals alike. If it gives spiritual relief to a single individual, it has been a success. If an adult feels validated because he or she realizes that the behaviors or qualities he or she dislikes or feels guilty about are actually survival skills learned unconsciously as a child in a dysfunctional family, then this book has served an important purpose. It is written in the context of talking about addiction because that has been my life's work and passion. However, I believe the basic human truths presented here can apply and be helpful to anyone, whether it be a family therapist, an addict in early recovery, a psychologist, or a busy parent. Life is a struggle, but taken one day at a time, being out of self, with a spiritual focus, it can also be a path of discovery through our pain to love, freedom, and peace.

# Also available from Central Recovery Press

www.centralrecoverypress.com

## Inspirational

*The Truth Begins with You: Reflections to Heal Your Spirit*
Claudia Black, PhD • $17.95 US • ISBN-13: 978-1-936290-61-1

*Above and Beyond: 365 Meditations for*
*Transcending Chronic Pain and Illness*
JS Dorian • $15.95 US • ISBN-13: 978-1-936290-66-6

*Guide Me in My Recovery: Prayers for Times of Joy and Times of Trial*
Rev. John T. Farrell, PhD • $12.95 US • ISBN-13: 978-1-936290-00-0
*Special hardcover gift edition*: $19.95 US • ISBN-13: 978-1-936290-02-4

*The Soul Workout: Getting and Staying Spiritually Fit*
Helen H. Moore • $12.95 US • ISBN-13: 978-0-9799869-8-7

*Tails of Recovery: Addicts and the Pets That Love Them*
Nancy A. Schenck • $19.95 US • ISBN-13: 978-0-9799869-6-3

*Of Character: Building Assets in Recovery*
Denise D. Crosson, PhD • $12.95 US • ISBN-13: 978-0-9799869-2-5

# Memoirs

*Leave the Light On: A Memoir of Recovery and Self-Discovery*
Jennifer Storm • $14.95 US • ISBN-13: 978-0-9818482-2-8

*The Mindful Addict: A Memoir of the Awakening of a Spirit*
Tom Catton • $18.95 US • ISBN-13: 978-0-9818482-7-3

*Becoming Normal: An Ever-Changing Perspective*
Mark Edick • $14.95 US • ISBN-13: 978-0-9818482-1-1

*Dopefiend: A Father's Journey from Addiction to Redemption*
Tim Elhajj • 16.95 US • ISBN 13: 978-1-936290-63-5